1

Learn to Listen
Listen to Learn

Academic Listening and Note-Taking

Third Edition

PEARSON
Longman

Roni S. Lebauer

Learn to Listen—Listen to Learn 1
Academic Listening and Note-Taking
Third Edition

Pearson Education, 10 Bank Street, White Plains, NY 10606

Staff credits: The people who made up the *Learn to Listen—Listen to Learn 1,*
   Third Edition team, representing editorial, production, design, and manufacturing are:
   Pietro Alongi, Rhea Banker, Dave Dickey, Françoise Leffler, Jaime Lieber,
   Amy McCormick, Linda Moser, Carlos Rountree, Jennifer Stem, and Paula Van Ells.

Cover design: Barbara Sabella
Text design: Word & Image Design
Text composition: Word & Image Design
Text font: ITC Giovanni

Library of Congress Cataloging-in-Publication Data
Lebauer, R. Susan.
   Learn to listen - listen to learn 1 : academic listening and note-taking / Roni S. Lebauer. — 3rd ed.
      p. cm.
   Includes bibliographical references and index.
   ISBN-13: 978-0-13-814001-4 (pbk.)
   ISBN-10: 0-13-814001-4 (pbk.)
   1. Lecture method in teaching. 2. Listening. 3. Note-taking. 4. English language—Study and teaching—
   United States—Foreign speakers. I. Title.
   LB2393.L43 2010
   371.39'6—dc22
                          2009010341

ISBN-10: 0-13-814001-4
ISBN-13: 978-0-13-814001-4

PEARSON LONGMAN ON THE **WEB**

Pearsonlongman.com offers online resources for teachers and students. Access our Companion Websites, our online catalog, and our local offices around the world.

Visit us at **www.pearsonlongman.com**.

Printed in the United States of America

CONTENTS

KV 03.15.2019 1416

PREFACE

This book is designed to help advanced ESL/EFL students prepare for the demands of academic lecture comprehension and note-taking.

Listening to lectures and taking notes involves more than language skills alone. Rather, lecture comprehension and note-taking require skills in **evaluating information** (deciding what is important and needs to be noted), **organizing information** (seeing how ideas relate to each other), and **predicting information** (anticipating the content and direction of a lecture). This book teaches these skills and also includes exercises focusing on the acquisition of vocabulary and the **recognition of language cues** (lexical, grammatical, and paralinguistic cues) that are used in lectures to signal lecture organization.

One goal of this book is to **teach students *how* to listen to a lecture and take notes:** how to recognize lecture organization, use lecture cues and conventions that indicate organization and emphasis, recognize redundancy, and predict information. The text teaches these skills and provides numerous opportunities to practice them.

Another goal of this book is to **provide materials that replicate the style and function of academic lectures.** The lectures in the text have been selected to motivate students to listen, not just to complete a language task but also to gain knowledge about a variety of topics. These lectures cover a wide range of fields, and are accessible to the layperson yet still of interest to the specialist. The text also aims to simulate the lecture situation by allowing teachers to either deliver the lectures live (using the outlines in the Teacher's Manual), play recorded lectures given by a variety of speakers, or both. In addition, many activities in the book include excerpts from lectures originally given to audiences comprising native English speakers.

KEY CHANGES IN THE THIRD EDITION

- The overall organization of the book has been changed to allow teachers and students to proceed through the book more sequentially.

- Lectures have been updated and new lectures and excerpts have been added. Lecture topics continue to reflect a diversity of disciplines, including the arts, humanities, sciences, engineering, technology, and social sciences.

- Explanations have been simplified.

- Strategies for listening, note-taking, and studying are emphasized.

- "Replay Questions" activities have been added, drawing attention to specific idioms, facts, or attitudes.

- "Other Voices" follow-up exercises have been added to each lecture, giving exposure and practice to interaction typical in university settings (e.g., questions in class, office visits, small group discussions, informal banter among students after class). Not only do these exercises give students listening practice, but they also give insight into expectations and behavior on U.S. campuses.

- Post-lecture comprehension checks have been revised and, in addition to questions about facts from the lecture, also include inference and attitude questions. The range of formats for comprehension checks has been expanded beyond True/False, multiple-choice, short-answer, and essay questions to include graphic organizers and sequencing questions.

- Because many students are interested in taking the TOEFL® iBT test (which includes a lecture comprehension portion), question types typical of that test are also included throughout the text.

- Vocabulary practice has been expanded with each lecture unit containing at least three opportunities to learn and practice vocabulary and vocabulary development strategies. Academic Word List vocabulary has been highlighted and is practiced in multiple activities. Vocabulary is often recycled among lectures and activities so that repeated exposure in different settings can strengthen acquisition.

- Extension activities have been revised to include a range of activities exploring what students might "do" with academic content: research, presentations, and web browsing, along with general reading, writing, speaking, and listening activities, all provide additional opportunities to personalize and expand upon ideas raised in the lectures.

How to Use This Book

The text is divided into nine units. Units build upon previous units and recycle information learned. Throughout the book, strategies for college success—particularly for improving listening, note-taking, study skills habits, and vocabulary development—are highlighted.

- Unit 1 is a pre-coursework evaluation, containing lectures and exercises that help the teacher evaluate students' levels prior to using this book (and help students self-evaluate and consider what they might need to concentrate on). The lecture in this section is related to study skills, and thus it informs as well as tests.

- **Unit 2** aims to increase student awareness of lecture discourse, with lecture transcripts and exercises demonstrating the high degree of paraphrase and redundancy in lectures and the use of cues that introduce topics, signal organization, and conclude lectures. Through awareness and practice, students gain an understanding of how important these discourse factors are, enabling them to predict ideas and lecture direction. In Unit 2, students are examining lecture discourse by reading and discussing transcripts of authentic lectures.

- **Unit 3** allows students to hear authentic excerpts from lectures originally given in university or conference settings. The activities focus on predicting and confirming lecture direction from introductions and conclusions. In addition, students learn to recognize when lecturers go "off track" with digressions and when they get back "on track."

- **Unit 4** begins note-taking practice and instruction; it contains guidelines, information, and exercises on note-taking basics: noting key words, using symbols, and using space on the page to show relationships between ideas.

- **Unit 5** contains lectures and exercises on noting numbers, years, and statistics.

- **Units 6, 7, and 8**, "Focus on Lecture Organization, Parts 1, 2 and 3," introduce students to different organizational plans used in lectures. The students then practice comprehending, predicting, and taking notes from lecture excerpts that demonstrate these organizational plans. (As in Unit 3, excerpt material is truly authentic, coming directly from transcripts of college or conference lectures, originally given to English-fluent speaking audiences.)

- **Unit 9** is a consolidation unit, tying together and reviewing skills and strategies learned throughout the book. It contains two lectures that can serve as a final evaluation. Students are given less guidance and preparation for listening and note-taking, and they can use their notes as they might in a university situation. That is, they put them aside and use them as a reference in preparation for a quiz one or two weeks later.

PRE- AND POST-LECTURE ACTIVITIES

In Units 6 through 8, activities generally occur in the following sequence:

- **Discipline or Topic-Related Vocabulary.** Students can review words they already know and learn additional words in order to expand their vocabulary and general information schema for the topic covered in the lecture.

- **Pre-Lecture Discussion.** This activity provides background information, elicits interest, and provides a vehicle for the introduction of relevant vocabulary. The discussion often revolves around readings related to the topic.

- **Preparing for the Lecture.** Students discuss their expectations of the lecture based on the lecture title and the Pre-Lecture Discussion. This helps students build additional background knowledge. It also helps them make predictions about lecture content and organization before listening. Often, an introductory excerpt is played to give students continued practice in recognizing topic introductions.

- **Listening for the Larger Picture.** Students listen to the lecture once without taking notes and then answer questions. This helps them focus on getting the larger picture without becoming preoccupied with details. This section employs language similar to that used in the TOEFL® iBT listening sections, asking students to explain how the speaker accomplishes his or her goal (e.g., by listing, by comparing).

- **Organization.** Students read a summary of the lecture organization to affirm their initial comprehension or guide them toward better comprehension.

- **Defining Vocabulary.** Students listen to vocabulary from the lecture in different contexts and choose the correct meaning. Words marked with an asterisk are included in the AWL Vocabulary List.*

- **Listening and Note-Taking.** Students listen to the lecture a second time and take notes. Minimal comments in the margin guide the students by giving information about the lecture organization, while at the same time allowing them to develop their own note-taking style. After that, they revise or rewrite their notes so that they are better organized and include all relevant information.

- **"Replay" Questions.** Students listen to short excerpts from the larger lecture. These questions—often similar to those used in the listening section of the TOEFL® iBT exam—target vocabulary, content, inferences, lecturer's attitudes, lecturer's purpose for giving specific information, and lecturer's means of accomplishing a goal.

- **"Other Voices" Follow-Up.** After lectures, students listen to segments (often conversations) that relate to classroom concerns or that follow up on ideas presented in the lecture. Whereas lectures are largely unidirectional with the lecturer doing most or all of the talking, these listening activities typically focus on different types of interaction that take place in and around university lectures. This includes office visits (for multiple purposes such as career guidance, discussion of difficulties, inquiries about grades, sharing of information), end-of-class questions, student-to-student discussions in and out of class, and media presentations (such as astronauts' audio clips). Questions in this section practice many skills tested in the listening section of the TOEFL® iBT exam and involve recognizing main topics, facts, speakers' purposes, attitudes, and methods.

---

* The Academic Word List was developed in 2000 by Averil Coxhead from a written academic corpus of material used in the fields of liberal arts, commerce, law, and science. It contains 570 words that appear most frequently in this corpus.

- **Post-Lecture Discussion.** Students participate in group discussions that encourage communication about issues raised in the lecture. Often these discussions involve additional related readings. This also serves to divert students' attention from the specific lecture details for a short while, forcing them to use their notes—rather than rely on memory—when doing the next activity.

- **Using Your Notes.** Students test the accuracy of their notes by using them to answer questions representative of those on university tests, such as True/False, multiple-choice, short-answer, and essay questions. In addition to recognition of stated information, students are asked to infer information and attitudes.

- **Comparing Ideas.** Students compare and discuss their notes to discover alternative and perhaps more effective ways to take notes.

- **Academic Word List Vocabulary.** These vocabulary exercises offer additional practice with academic vocabulary, derivations, and synonyms.

- **Using Vocabulary.** Students practice new vocabulary in different contexts, including conversational ones.

- **Retaining Vocabulary.** Using words employed in the lecture and activities, a specific vocabulary retention strategy is suggested and practiced.

- **Extension Activities.** Students use information from the lecture and related reading(s) in an extension Speaking and Listening Activity (such as a presentation or debate); a Writing Activity (such as an essay or letter); or a Reading/Research activity (such as Web site explorations and reports).

ANCILLARY MATERIALS

Audio CDs and a Teacher's Manual accompany this text.

- The **Audio CDs** provide exposure to a variety of speaking styles and can be a valuable resource for work in the classroom or language laboratory.

- The **Teacher's Manual** contains teaching suggestions, lecture outlines, lecture transcripts, exercise transcripts, and answer keys. It also has quizzes for the lectures in Unit 9.

Guidelines for Presenting Lectures

This book has been designed for maximum flexibility. Depending on the needs and expectations of their students, teachers have two options for presenting lectures. One option is to use the CDs, which allow teachers to expose students to a number of speaking styles and accents. Another option is for teachers to present live lectures to the class. To assist teachers in presenting lectures naturally, lecture outlines are included in the Teacher's Manual. The outlines give the basic information and structure of the lectures; it is up to the teacher to paraphrase, repeat, add information, go off on tangents, and summarize as necessary. The Teacher's Manual also includes transcripts of the recorded lectures to show how the lectures could sound when presented.

Live delivery of the lectures by ESL/EFL teachers cannot, of course, be completely authentic. Research has shown that ESL/EFL teachers adapt their language to fit the level of their nonnative speaker audiences. Although it may be impossible to completely erase all such "teacher talk" from lecture delivery, teachers should be aware of whether and how much they adapt their language. The goal should be to help students listen to lectures as they would be presented to native speaker listeners. Therefore, teachers should aim for their usual rate of speaking, vocabulary, and amount of repetition and paraphrase.

Notes on the "Authenticity" of Lectures

Lecture excerpts in Units 3, 6, 7, and 8 are truly authentic; that is, they were originally given by lecturers who were speaking to a native-English-proficient audience and who were unaware that their lectures would later be used for language teaching purposes. These lectures were transcribed verbatim and rerecorded professionally.

Longer lectures in this text have a different kind of authenticity. These lectures were delivered from outlines, not scripts, by native speakers to audiences composed of native and non-native English speakers. Lecturers were encouraged to speak naturally, but being aware that some in the audience were not fluent English speakers, they likely made some adaptations to their style. These lectures were recorded on site, transcribed, and later rerecorded professionally.

Together, these listening experiences expose students to material that is both accessible and authentic.

ACKNOWLEDGMENTS

Several people have helped me bring this book and its previous editions to its present form, and each of them deserves my sincere thanks:

- Miho Steinberg and Richard Day for first giving me release time from teaching duties in order to develop materials for an advanced ESL listening comprehension course;
- Ted Plaister and David Rickard for their encouragement of my work in listening comprehension and for providing technical resources and ideas that, way back then, provided stimuli for the first edition of this book;
- Ellen Broidy, Robert Ferguson, Michael Merrifield, Morgan Barrow, Larry Perez, Karah Street, Timothy Braatz and the many other professors and speakers whose lectures and office visits I transcribed and used to examine lecture discourse and create many of the exercises in this book;
- Robin Scarcella and Vicki Bergman-Lanier for providing me with opportunities to pilot my original materials in their programs;
- The teachers who took extra time from their usually busy schedules to test this latest edition and previous versions and provide feedback: Aaron Albright, Martha Compton, Janice Jensen, Matthew Hunt, Lorraine Kumpf, Barbara Luthor, Wendy Maccoun, Kathy Smith, Susan Stern, Judy Tanka, Judy Via, and Angeliki Volksman;
- Colleagues and friends who provided creative and intellectual support: Jeanne Mazique, Jeffrey Clark, Michael Thorstensen, Jan Barber;
- The editorial and production teams at Pearson Education for their enthusiasm, talent, and professionalism, along with Dorothy Zemach for her creativity, competence, and encouragement;
- The many anonymous reviewers and users whose thoughtful comments helped me revise and revise and revise;
- And finally, Michelle Rene-Ryan for being herself and being part of my life.

Roni S. Lebauer

CREDITS

Listening Selections and Text

Unit 1, Lecture 1: Hopper, Carolyn H. 2007. *Practicing College Learning Strategies*, 4th edition. New York: Houghton Mifflin. Thayer, Robert E. "Energy walks: don't touch that candy bar. A short walk gives you a longer energy boost and improves your mood." *Psychology Today* 22 (10), October 1988, p. 12. Thayer, Robert E. 1996. *The Origin of Everyday Moods*. New York: Oxford University Press.

Unit 3 Lecture Excerpts: Tal Ben-Shahar, Harvard University. "Positive Psychology: Psych 1504." William T Greenough. "Use It or Lose It: Brain Plasticity across the Lifespan." Irvine Health Foundation Lecture Series, Feb. 5, 1997. Robert Ferguson, Saddleback College. "Intro to Psychology: Psych 1." Lawrence Perez, Saddleback College. "Pre-Algebra: Math 351." Ellen

Broidy, University of California, Irvine Research Librarian. "Topic Analysis."

Unit 4, Lecture 2: "Chinese language just for women." Washington Post, MSNBC.com. http://www.msnbc.msn.com/id/4356095/from!ET/. Watts, Jon. "The forbidden tongue," *The Guardian* (September 23, 2005). http://www.guardian.co.uk/world/2005/sep/23/china.gender.

Unit 5, Lecture 3: Harris Poll #120, Dec. 4, 2007. "Pets are 'members of the family' and 2/3 of pet owners buy their pets holiday presents." http://www.harrisinteractive.com/harris_poll/index.asp?PID=840. "China: changing attitudes to pet ownership drive pet food sales," *Euromonitor International*. http://www.marketresearchworld.net/index.php?option=content&task=view&id=281sitemid.

Unit 5, Lecture 4: "History of Tobacco." Boston University Medical Center, Community Outreach Health Info System. http://academic.udayton.edu/health/syllabi/tobacco/history.htm. © 1993-2007 Gene Borio, Tobacco BBS. http://www.tobacco.org/resources/history/Tobacco_History.html. "A Brief History of Tobacco." http://www.cnn.com/US/9705/tobacco/history/index.html.

Unit 6 Lecture Excerpts: Tal Ben-Shahar, Harvard University. "Positive Psychology: Psych 1504." Robert Ferguson, Saddleback College. "Intro to Psychology: Psych 1." Ellen Broidy, University of California, Irvine Research Librarian. "Topic Analysis." James McGaugh, Director, Center for the Neurobiology of Learning and Memory and Research, Professor, Department of Neurobiology and Behavior, UC Irvine. "The Magic of Memory: Peeking Behind the Brain's Curtain." Irvine Health Foundation Lecture Series, May 22, 2002. http://www.ihf.org/resources/2002_lectures/mcgaugh_trans.htm; Jeremy Wolfe, MIT OpenCourseWare. "Intro to Psych," Fall 2004. **Unit 6, Lecture 5:** Greening, Tom, and Dick Hobson. 1979. *Instant Relief: The Encyclopedia of Self-Help*, pp. 329–352. New York: Simon and Schuster. Holmes, T., and R.H. Rahe. "The social readjustment rating scale," reprinted from *Journal of Psychosomatic Research*, Vol. 11 (1967), with permission from Elsevier Science. **Unit 6, Lecture 6:** Kormandy, E.J. 1984. *Concepts of Ecology*, 3rd ed., pp. 274–277. Englewood Cliffs, NJ: Prentice Hall Inc. LaBastille, Anne. "The international acid test," *Sierra* (May/June 1986), p. 51. Reprinted with permission of *Sierra*. Nebel, Bernard J., and Richard T. Wright. 1996. *The Way the World Works: Environmental Science*, 5th ed., pp. 382–385; 400–408. Upper Saddle River, NJ: Prentice Hall Inc.

Unit 7 Lecture Excerpts: Steve Meier, University of Idaho. "Psych 372." Robert Ferguson, Saddleback College. "Psych 1 Intro to Psychology." Michael Merrifield, Saddleback College. "Anthro 2." Jan Chipchase. "Our Cell Phones: Ourselves," TED lecture series, March 2007. Dr. Robert Stickgold. "Sleep, Memory and Dreams: What are they good for?" Irvine Health Foundation Lecture Series, March 16, 2004. © 1980 Science Digest, "Project 1: Dinosaur Footprints" and "Project 2: Search for Neanderthals" are sponsored by the nonprofit Earthwatch Institute, http://www.earthwatch.org. Reprinted by permission. Ellen Broidy, UC Irvine Research Librarian. "Topic Analysis." **Unit 7, Lecture 7:** Crosher, Judith. *Ancient Egypt*. 1993. New York: Penguin Group. Ingber Stein, Dina. "New tools unearth the past," *Science Digest* (Nov–Dec. 1980), pp. 99–101. Reprinted by permission. Millard, Anne. 1996. *Pyramids*. New York: Larousse Kingfisher Chambers Inc. **Unit 7, Lecture 8:** Blair, Gwenda. "Researchers sniff out pheromones," *Los Angeles Times* (Dec. 29, 1997), pp. S1, S4. Copyright © 1997 Los Angeles Times. Reprinted by permission. Shorey, H. H. 1976. *Animal Communication by Pheromones*. New York: Academic Press.

Unit 8 Lecture Excerpts: Tal Ben-Shahar, Harvard University. "Positive Psychology: Psych 1504." Michael Merrifield, Saddleback College. "Anthro 2." Brian Shelton, Rock Valley College. "Silent Film Era Film History and Appreciation." Steve Meier, University of Idaho. "Psych 372." **Unit 8, Lecture 9:** Carpenter, Susan. "Gearing up for the new race to space," *Los Angeles Times* (June 23, 1998), pp. E1, E5. Cernan, Eugene. 2000. Interview. *To the Moon*. Courtesy of NOVA/WGBH Boston. Copyright © 1999 WGBH Educational Foundation. http://www.pbs.org/wgbh/nova/tothemoon/cernan.html. Cole, K.C. "Water possibly found on moon," *Los Angeles Times* (March 6, 1998), pp. A1, A18. Dixon, Robert T. *Dynamic Astronomy*, pp. 151–160. Englewood Cliffs, NJ: Prentice Hall Inc. Kelley, Kevin W. (Ed.). 1988. *The Home Planet*. Reading, MA: Addison Wesley. Thornton, Jeannye. "Moon rooms?" *U.S. News & World Report* (June 1, 1998), p. 12. Copyright © 1998, U.S. News & World Report. Reprinted by permission. **Unit 8, Lecture 10:** Hamlin, Suzanne. "Science may help green tea get steeped in U.S. culture," *The OC Register* (June 30, 1994), p. 9. "Reading tea leaves for health benefits," *Tufts University Diet and Nutrition Letter*, 13:8 (October 1995), p. 4. Reprinted with permission: Tufts Health & Nutrition Letter. "Can green tea help prevent cancer?" *University of California at Berkeley Wellness Letter*, 14:3 (Dec. 1997), pp. 1–2.

Unit 9, Lecture 11: Cole, K.C. "Vetoing the way America votes," *Los Angeles Times* (August 16, 1995), pp. A1, A10. Copyright © 1995 Los Angeles Times. Reprinted by permission. Burns, James M., J.W. Peltason, and Thomas E. Cronin. 1985. *Government by the People*, 12th alt. ed., pp. 195–199. Englewood Cliffs, NJ: Prentice Hall Inc. **Unit 9, Lecture 12:** Crosher, Judith. 1993. *Ancient Egypt*. New York: Penguin Group. Maugh, Thomas H., II. "World's oldest paved road found in Egypt," *Los Angeles Times* (May 7, 1997), p. A14. Copyright © 1997 Los Angeles Times. Reprinted by permission. Millard, Anne. 1996. *Pyramids*. New York: Larousse Kingfisher Chambers Inc.

Photos

Pages 28, 47, 154 Shutterstock. **Page 56** The Mariners' Museum, Newport News, VA. **Page 108** AP Photo/The Daily Times, Marc F. Henning. **Page 113** Fotolia.com **Page 114** American Museum of Natural History. **Page 142** NASA Headquarters. **Page 179** (t), Corbis Digital Stock; (c), Adalberto Rios/Photodisc, Inc.; (b), CORBIS/Marilyn Bridges.

Illustrations

Pages 1, 2, 74, 86, 169 Dusan Petricic. **Pages 9, 10, 13, 23, 31, 32, 40, 41, 65, 97, 105, 120, 131, 142, 170** Andy Myer. **Page 149** Designed by Peter Inston—London. **Page 156** Copyright © The New Yorker Collection, 1979. Sidney Harris from cartoonbank.com. All Rights Reserved. **Page 167** Ken Batelman.

STARTING OUT: PRE-COURSEWORK EVALUATION

Goals

- Evaluate listening comprehension skills
- Evaluate note-taking skills
- Evaluate ability to note numbers

DISCUSSION

Study Habits

1. Where do you study? How long do you study in a sitting? Do you take breaks when you study? What do you do during your breaks? Do you have a regular daily or weekly study schedule or do you "fit studying in" when you can?

2. Do you like a certain environment for studying? For example, do you listen to music while you study or do you prefer quiet? Do you study with classmates or by yourself?

3. Do you have techniques for remembering information? What kinds of techniques do you use?

4. How well do you remember and retain vocabulary? What techniques help you most? Share those with your classmates.

5. What aspects of your study habits work well for you?

6. What would you like to improve about your study habits?

 A

Evaluating Listening Comprehension and Note-Taking Skills

Learners benefit by reflecting on their strengths and weaknesses. This helps them focus their study efforts. Similarly, teachers need to get a sense of their students' goals, strengths, and weaknesses so they can focus their teaching efforts. For both, it is important to be able to measure progress, and understanding one's starting point is an essential first step.

In this unit, you will listen to two parts of a short lecture about effective study skills and habits and then a dictation of numbers. You will practice taking notes and using your notes to complete a chart and answer comprehension questions. After each activity, you will evaluate your listening comprehension and note-taking ability. To get a sense of your listening and note-taking skills, your teacher will also evaluate your notes and your answers.

LECTURE 1

Study Tips (Psychology)

ACTIVITY 1   LISTENING AND NOTE-TAKING (PART 1)

🎧 The first part of the lecture focuses on the study technique of "recitation." (If you do not know the word "recitation," listen for what the lecturer tells you about it.) Take notes below (or on a separate piece of paper) as if you were in a class and responsible for the material covered in the lecture.

Did you know?

The human brain is comprised of more than 100 billion cells.

Study Tips, Part 1

Self-Evaluation

1. Describe your ability to comprehend this part of the lecture.

____ Excellent   ____ Very Good   ____ Good   ____ Fair   ____ Poor

2. Describe your ability to take notes while listening to this part of the lecture.

____ Excellent   ____ Very Good   ____ Good   ____ Fair   ____ Poor

The second part of the lecture discusses studies on ways to boost mood and energy. Take notes on a separate piece of paper as if you were in a class and responsible for the material covered in the lecture

> Study Tips, Part 2

Self-Evaluation

1. Describe your ability to comprehend this part of the lecture.

    —— Excellent —— Very Good —— Good —— Fair —— Poor

2. Describe your ability to take notes while listening to this part of the lecture.

    —— Excellent —— Very Good —— Good —— Fair —— Poor

ACTIVITY **3** **USING YOUR NOTES**

Use your notes from the lecture in this unit to answer the questions below.

PART 1:

1. What is "recitation"?

    _____

2. Recitation works for three reasons. What are those reasons?

    a. _____

    b. _____

    c. _____

3. What are three ways the lecturer suggests for applying recitation to studying?

    a. _____

    b. _____

    c. _____

PART 2:

4. Who is Robert Thayer?

    _____

5. Fill in the following chart with information about Thayer's four studies.

	Research Question	Participants	Procedure	Results/Findings
Study #1	How does _____ affect _____?		1. Participants filled out a checklist rating feelings of energy/tension 2. 3.	
Study #2				
Study #3				
Study #4				

Self-Evaluation

1. Describe the usefulness and accuracy of your notes when answering these questions.

   ___ Excellent   ___ Very Good   ___ Good   ___ Fair   ___ Poor

2. If you want to take more useful and more accurate notes, what do you need to work on?

   _____

   _____

Discuss the following questions in small groups.

1. Consider the suggestions made in this lecture. What do you already do? What might you want to try? What do you think would not work for you and why?

2. How do you typically give yourself an energy or mood boost? Do the findings of the studies fit your experience? Do you have any other "tips"?

ACTIVITY **5** **DICTATION OF NUMBERS: AN EVALUATION**

Numbers, statistics, and dates are frequently heard in lectures in many disciplines. It is important, again, that you and your teacher reflect on and evaluate your current ability to comprehend and note numbers.

🎧 **Listen to statements containing numbers. Write the numbers that you hear.**

1. Michelangelo was born in _____.

2. Mary Wollstonecraft Shelley, English author (*Frankenstein*), was born in _____ and died in _____.

3. 1 cup raisins = _____ calories

4. _____ grams of yogurt from partially skimmed milk = _____ calories

5. In _____, _____ of immigrants to the United States were from Asia.

6. The Missouri River is _____ miles long.

7. Mount Everest is _____ feet high.

8. The total surface area of Antarctica is _____ square miles in summer, _____ the size of Australia.

9. India's population is projected to be _____ in _____.

10. Tokyo's projected population in 2025 is _____.

11. A tsunami occurred in Aceh, Indonesia, on _____.

12. The tsunami was caused by an underwater earthquake measuring _____ on the Richter Scale, resulting in _____ deaths.

13. In a survey taken in _____ asking people about problems in their country, nearly _____ people in India said "pollution."

14. In the year _____, oil consumption varied: China consumed a little less than _____ of U.S. consumption; Brazil consumed about _____ the amount that the United States did.

15. Length of board = _____ feet; width = _____ inches; depth = _____ inches

16. One pound = _____ grams

Self-Evaluation

When you have finished the dictation, answer the following questions.

1. Describe your ability to note the numbers.

   ___ Excellent   ___ Very Good   ___ Good   ___ Fair   ___ Poor

2. What kind of numbers were hardest for you to note? dates? the ~*teen* versus ~*ty* ending such as *17* and *70*? large numbers? fractions (such as $\frac{1}{3}$)? percentages (*53 percent*)? ratios (*1 in 6*)? decimals (*3.14*)?

B Teacher's Note-Taking Feedback Form

Your teacher will use a form similar to the one below when commenting on your notes in this class.

Note-Taking Feedback Form

Name _____

Date _____   Lecture _____

ORGANIZATION OF IDEAS[1]

____   You organize while you write. Good.

____   Your notes visually represent the relationship between ideas. Good.

____   Your notes reflect some attempt at visually representing the relationship between ideas. Keep working on that.

____   Your notes are unclear; it is not possible to quickly see the relationship between ideas. Work on organizing your notes so that the important ideas stand out and the relationships between ideas are clear. Use the space on the page to show how pieces of information relate to other pieces of information (through indenting or connecting lines, for example). Use headings to show how ideas relate to one another.

____   Your notes reflect random noting of words. Evaluate as you listen to get the main points first. Add details when you have time or when rewriting notes.

____   You seem to be trying to note down every word. Focus on noting the minimum number of "key words" that would carry the same meaning. This will allow you more time during listening and note-taking for comprehending and evaluating ideas.

Additional comments about organization:

_____

_____

_____

(continued on next page)

[1] Unit 4 introduces the ideas of noting key words and organizing notes while listening.

ACCURACY AND COMPLETENESS OF NOTES

_____ You seem to get most points, both major and minor. Good.

_____ You seem to get most points (especially the major ones) but miss or misinterpret (a few / many) minor ones. It's good that you are able to discriminate between major ideas and minor ones. Practice and increased fluency in English will help you note more details.

_____ You miss or misinterpret (a few / many) major ideas and (a few / many) minor ideas. Focus on getting the major points first. When you have time, note details related to these major points.

_____ You may be noting too few "key words." These notes would probably not be helpful later. Revise or rewrite your notes as soon as possible after lectures so that you can expand your notes with information that you remember.

Additional comments about accuracy and completeness of notes:

_____

_____

_____

ACCURACY OF NOTING NUMBERS[2]

_____ You seem to be able to note most numbers. Good.

_____ You miss or misinterpret a few numbers.

_____ You miss or misinterpret many numbers.

Additional comments about accuracy of noting numbers:

_____

_____

_____

OVERALL EVALUATION

_____

_____

_____

_____

_____

_____

_____

_____

_____

_____

_____

[2] Unit 5, in particular, focuses on noting numbers.

UNDERSTANDING LECTURE DESIGN

Goals

- Increase awareness of lecture design
- Increase ability to predict content and organizational direction in lectures

DISCUSSION

Language

1. Do you prefer to read or to listen for information? Is one easier for you than the other? If so, why? Is this the same in your native language?

2. What are some differences between listening to a lecture and reading the same information in a textbook?

3. What makes listening to lectures difficult in a second language? What makes it difficult in your native language?

4. Talk about the languages you have learned or studied. What do you feel comfortable or uncomfortable doing in each language (e.g., talking to friends, talking and listening on the phone, writing e-mail, writing academic papers, reading the newspaper, reading textbooks)?

A Comparing the Language of Lecturing to the Language of Writing

Imagine you are reading a linguistics textbook. The subject is how people use language to achieve their goals. You read this paragraph:

> One way to look at language is from a sociological or sociolinguistic perspective. In this view, language is seen as a game in which each person in a particular language community knows all the rules. Unlike recreational games, however, this game is taken very seriously.

 Now listen to a lecturer *telling* you the same information. Here are the words that a professor actually used in a classroom:

Let's first look at one aspect of language . . . I want to look at the sociological or sociolinguistic way of looking at language . . . all right . . . from this point of view some linguists have come up with the idea that language is a game . . . like football, soccer, baseball . . . each person who speaks in any particular language or any community knows all the rules of this game . . . they know how to play . . . somebody who comes from a different one . . . as you know well . . . may not know all the rules . . . so you have some problems with communication . . . now because we said language is a game doesn't necessarily mean that we play it for fun . . . we usually play it for serious reasons . . . most of the time . . . although sometimes we tell jokes and things like that . . . hmmm . . . I seem to do that quite often in this class . . . but the rules . . . no matter what we do . . . are very well defined . . . you may not know what they are . . . but they're very clear rules of what you can do and what you can't do in any situation . . .

There is a big difference between the two, yet the information in the textbook and the lecture is basically the same.

Exercise

Compare the lecture excerpt to the textbook paragraph. Write down the ways that they differ.

TEXTBOOK PARAGRAPH	LECTURE EXCERPT

 Recognizing Cues

CUES TO TOPIC INTRODUCTIONS

When you compared the language used in a textbook to the language used in a lecture, you may have noticed that, in the lecture excerpt, you are given explicit (stated) directions about what to listen for.

Example

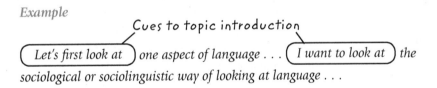

Cues to topic introduction

(Let's first look at) one aspect of language . . . (I want to look at) *the sociological or sociolinguistic way of looking at language . . .*

We can call these directions **cues**. They direct you to listen to something. The words noted in the example are **cues to topic introductions**. Some cues to topic introductions are specific, such as *Let's look at X*. Other topic introduction cues may not be as specific, but they still give you a hint that the speaker is starting a new idea. For example, the expressions *All right* and *Now* sometimes indicate a topic introduction.

Example

Possible cue to topic introduction

(All right) . . . *from this point of view some linguists have come up with the idea that language is a game . . .*

In written text, these cues to topic introductions are not needed, for a couple of reasons. First, written text is permanent. The reader can reread the words to better understand what the writer is trying to say. Second, written text is organized so that paragraphs generally focus on one main idea. The reader can find main ideas by looking for topic sentences or thesis statements. The indentation of a new paragraph generally tells the reader that a new idea is beginning.

In contrast, speakers can use their tone of voice and intonation to indicate a topic introduction. They might pause before introducing the topic or emphasize signal words and phrases such as "All right" or "Now."

LISTENING AND NOTE-TAKING STRATEGY

Listen for cues to topic introductions. Some are specific, such as *Let's look at X*, *Today we're going to talk about X*, or *Let's move on to X*. Others may not be as specific (*All right*, *Now*), but they can still give you a hint that the speaker is starting a new idea.

You will learn more about these cues in Unit 3.

CUES TO ORGANIZATION

When writers write, they consider how they can organize their ideas in order to present them most clearly. Writers use phrases such as *the first example*, *the second point*, *on the other hand*, and so on. Lecturers also use these **cues to organization** so that their listeners can more easily understand their ideas and how they relate to each other.

Example

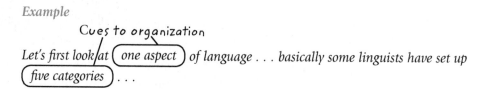

Let's first look at (one aspect) of language . . . basically some linguists have set up (five categories) . . .

What do you expect the lecturer to do later on in this lecture?

These cues to organization help you make predictions about how the lecture will be organized. This, then, helps you plan your note-taking. For example, after hearing the lecturer mention *five categories*, a good note-taker would start a numbered list from one to five.

Notice how many cues to organization are in the next excerpt from the same lecture on language.

Basically some linguists have set up (five categories) of accomplishing things . . . we use language to describe . . . tell about the world that we see . . . there's a chair over there . . . there's a person over here . . . someone is from China . . . or whatever . . . (another thing) that we use it for is to tell people to do something . . . please close the door . . . please open the door . . . do your homework . . . do this . . . do that . . . now we might not always say do it but we have ways of telling people to do something . . . (another way) . . . (a third way) . . . is we use language to tell people what we're going to do . . . I'm going to tell you about language . . . I'm going to open the door . . . (another way) to look at language is to tell about feelings . . . express what's inside of us about the world . . . not only that there is a chair but that I don't like that chair or I do like that chair . . . and (the fifth way) or (the fifth thing) we use is to change the world . . . certain things that you say change the world . . . if I say you fail this course . . . that language changes the world . . . just my four words make you unhappy and hate me . . . something has changed because of my words and nothing else except those words . . . so we can change the world with language . . . now since we have all these different purposes and you probably can think of other purposes with which we want to use language to win or accomplish what we want inside . . . so it's kind of like a game that way.

LISTENING AND NOTE-TAKING STRATEGY

Listen for cues to organization. These cues will help you make predictions about what the lecturer will say. This will help you organize your notes and decide what is important to write down.

In Units 6, 7, and 8, you will learn more about specific cues to organization.

CUES TO TOPIC CONCLUSIONS

Look back at the lecture excerpt that you just read. Notice that when the lecturer has finished describing the five categories, she then attempts to tie the preceding ideas together by saying, "now since we have all these different purposes and you probably can think of other purposes with which we want to use language to win or accomplish what we want inside . . . so it's kind of like a game that way."

What kind of cues were used to indicate this topic completion?

- The speaker used reference words to group all the preceding information together by saying, "We have *all these different purposes*." This indicated a break from her previous goal of describing each of the five categories.
- She preceded the summary with a pause and the cue "now." (*Now* may indicate the beginning of a summary or a new idea.)
- Finally, the lecturer emphasized the conclusion of that topic in the last line, "so it's kind of like a game that way." Words such as *so*, *therefore*, and *thus* often signal a topic conclusion.

LISTENING AND NOTE-TAKING STRATEGY

Listen for cues telling you that the speaker is finishing an idea. Listen for a conclusion or a summary. If the lecture is not over, get ready for a new topic introduction.

You will learn more about cues to conclusions in Unit 3.

 C | # Recognizing Paraphrase, Repetition, Exemplification, and Digression

Have you ever heard anyone read aloud from a textbook or a journal article (or any piece of writing that was originally meant to be read silently)? It is often very difficult to follow. That is because in written language there is much less repetition and paraphrase than in spoken language.

This is a very important difference between the language of lectures and the language of writing. When writing, writers need to state an idea only once because they know that the readers can reread an idea many times. However, when listening, words can "go in one ear and out the other," so the lecturer must give the listeners time to think about or take notes on what they have heard. Lecturers do this by
- repeating their ideas in different ways (i.e., paraphrasing)
- repeating their ideas in exactly the same words
- expanding on their ideas in greater detail (e.g., by giving examples —exemplification).

Paraphrase, **repetition**, and **exemplification** do not add new ideas; they simply give the listener time to better understand the speaker's ideas. They let listeners know that the lecturer thinks a particular idea or concept is important. Although paraphrases and repetitions do not need to be noted a second time, it is sometimes useful for note-takers to note examples if there is time.

Lecturers also **digress**, or go off the topic, more often than writers do. This is because lectures are live events, and lecturers may express unplanned thoughts while speaking. In addition, lecturers often try to connect with their audience in a more personal way, and this may result in a digression. Writers can remove their digressions when they realize they are off topic; lecturers cannot. (Note-takers can use the time during digressions to listen and take a break from note-taking.)

Exercise 2

Listen to and reexamine the excerpt from the lecture about a sociolinguistic perspective on language. Work with a partner and label each of the highlighted expressions as a *repetition, paraphrase, digression,* or *example.* The first one has been done for you.

Let's first look at one aspect of language . . . I want to look at the sociological or sociolinguistic way of looking at language . . . all right . . . from this point of view some linguists have come up with the idea that language is a game . . .

[example] —— *like football, soccer, baseball . . . each person who speaks in any particular language or any community knows all the rules of this game . . . they know how to play*

[   ] *. . . somebody who comes from a different one . . . as you know well . . . may not know all the rules . . . so you have some problems with communication . . . now because we said language is a game doesn't necessarily mean that we play it for fun . . . we usually play it for serious reasons . . . most of the time*

[   ] *. . . although sometimes we tell jokes and things like that . . . hmmm . . . I seem to do that quite often in this class . . . but the rules . . . no matter what we do*

[   ] *. . . are very well defined . . . you may not know what they are . . . but they're . . . very clear rules of what you can do and what you can't do in any situation . . .*

LISTENING AND NOTE-TAKING STRATEGY

Lecturers spend a lot of time paraphrasing, repeating, exemplifying, and digressing. Use this time to decide what is important and what to note.

Summarizing Key Differences between the Language of Lecturing and the Language of Writing

Exercise 3

There are many differences between the language used for lecturing and the language used for writing. Review the differences and check your understanding of these ideas by writing *written* or *spoken* in the spaces below:

- _____ language uses punctuation to separate and relate ideas; _____ language uses a type of vocal punctuation (e.g., hesitations and intonation) to achieve the same purpose.

- _____ language often indicates new ideas by beginning new paragraphs. In _____ language, lecturers use verbal and nonverbal cues to indicate the introduction of new ideas, a change of topic, the conclusion of an idea, and the intended organization. Listeners depend on these cues to follow the lecture.

- _____ language typically has more paraphrasing, repetition, and exemplification than _____ language. This gives listeners more time to process important information. In addition, in _____ language, digressions are more likely because new thoughts arise while lecturers are speaking.

Exercise 4

The purpose of this exercise is to identify cues and extra information in a lecture excerpt. This can help you understand the overall organization and recognize the main ideas. The following excerpt includes both parts of the lecture about a sociolinguistic perspective on language that we have already examined.

Directions

1. Listen to and read the entire excerpt. Try to get a sense of what the lecturer is saying.

2. Circle all the cues.

3. Cross out all repetitions, paraphrases, examples, and digressions.

4. When you have finished, compare your choices with those of a classmate. Discuss why you marked what you did. Your answers do not have to be the same, but you should be able to explain why you marked the excerpt the way you did. The first half of the exercise has been done for you.

(Let's first look at) (one aspect) of language . . . (I want to look at) the sociological or sociolinguistic way of looking at language . . . (all right) . . from this point of view some linguists have come up with the idea that language is a game . . . ~~like football, soccer, baseball~~ . . . each person who speaks in any particular language or any community knows all the rules of this game . . . ~~they know how to play~~ . . . somebody who comes from a different one . . . as you know well . . . may not know all the rules . . . so you have some problems with communication . . (now) because we said language is a game doesn't necessarily mean that we play it for fun . . . we usually play it for serious reasons . . . most of the time . . . ~~although sometimes we tell jokes and things like that . . . hmmm . . . I seem to do that quite often in this class~~ . . . but the rules . . . no matter what we do . . . are very well defined . . . ~~you may not know what they are . . . but they're very clear rules of what you can do and what you can't do in any situation~~ . . . usually in any use of language people are trying to accomplish something . . . ~~trying to do something~~ . . . that's why they talk . . . ~~sometimes you just talk to yourself for no reason . . . some crazy people talk for no reason but most people talk because they want to accomplish something~~ . . . basically some linguists have set up (five categories) of accomplishing things . . . we use language to describe . . . tell about the world that we see . . . there's a chair over there . . . there's a person over here . . . someone is from China . . . or whatever . . . another thing that we use it for is to tell people to do something . . . please close the door . . . please open the door . . . do your homework . . . do this . . . do that . . . now we might not always say do it but we have ways of telling people to do something . . . another way . . . a third way . . . is we use language to tell people what we're going to do . . . I'm going to tell you about language . . . I'm going to open the door . . . another way to look at language . . . is to tell about feelings . . . express what's inside of us about the world . . . not only that there is a chair but that I don't like that chair or I do like that chair . . . and the fifth way or the fifth thing we use is to change the world . . . certain things that you say change the world . . . if I say you fail this course . . . that language changes the world . . . just my four words make you unhappy and hate me . . . something has changed because of my words and nothing else except those words . . . so we can change the world with language . . . now since we have all these different purposes and you probably can think of other purposes with which we want to use language to win or accomplish what we want inside . . . so it's kind of like a game that way.

E   Getting the Main Ideas Using Context and Prediction

Listeners use the cues in lectures to predict how the lecture is going to continue. They also **use the context to predict** missing words and ideas.

To understand the main ideas, you do not need to understand every word. While listening to a lecture, it is easy to miss words because your mind wanders, you are busy taking notes, you misunderstand something, or you do not know the vocabulary. However, this does not mean that you cannot understand the main ideas of the lecture. You can use logic, your knowledge of the subject, and lecture cues to make good guesses about what you might have missed.

Exercise 5

The purpose of this exercise is to demonstrate that you can get the main ideas of a lecture even if you do not understand every word and idea. The following excerpt is a later part of the lecture about a sociolinguistic perspective on language. Many words and ideas have been omitted. In some cases, you may be able to guess what has been left out; in other cases, you may not be sure.

Directions

1. Listen to and read the entire excerpt. Try to get an idea of what it is about. Do not spend time trying to figure out the missing word(s); just try to understand the main ideas.

2. Answer the question that follows the lecture.

3. Compare your answers with those of a classmate.

Now language is also like a game in a number of other ways . . . basically like a game . . . you usually need more than ▆▆▆▆▆▆▆ person to play language . . . usually ▆▆▆▆▆▆ talk to somebody else or ▆▆▆▆▆▆ group of people . . . sometimes you talk to yourself but that's more ▆▆▆▆▆▆▆ than usual except if you're thinking not outright talking . . . it's a game because it's ▆▆▆▆▆▆▆ . . . something that we ▆▆▆▆▆▆ together . . . another way it's like a ▆▆▆▆▆ is that the players ▆▆▆▆▆▆ . . . one person ▆▆▆▆▆▆ and a new person comes into the ▆▆▆▆▆▆ . . . three or four people are standing together . . . they may all be playing . . . one may leave and a substitute ▆▆▆▆▆▆ . . . so it's like a game in that way . . . another thing is of course like I said, you're out to win something just like ▆▆▆▆▆▆▆▆▆▆ . . . we're usually out to accomplish something . . . something tangible . . . or something intangible . . . like emotional satisfaction . . . something to that effect . . . okay . . . another thing is that everybody has his own style of ▆▆▆▆▆▆ like ▆▆▆▆▆▆▆▆▆▆ . . . just like that some speakers are very good at certain ways of speaking and have certain individual styles of speaking . . . everybody is ▆▆▆▆▆▆ . . . nobody speaks the same . . . also, like a soccer player or like any game player you can change your style . . . ▆▆▆▆▆▆▆▆▆ . . . so styles change as well as the fact that each person has his own style . . . all right and the last thing is that we have rules for the game . . . just like we have rules now in the classroom . . . when I talk, you ▆▆▆▆▆▆ unless I give you some signal that says it's time for you to talk or I stop talking . . . there are very definite rules for not interrupting and ▆▆▆▆▆▆▆ . . . and for all kinds of things . . . we all know these rules but we probably ▆▆▆▆▆▆▆▆▆ . . . . when you're talking about football you can say it's played in a field so big, so wide . . . you can't kick the ball off the field . . . it has many rules and everybody can learn those ▆▆▆▆▆▆ and tell us what they are . . . language is a little different . . . if I asked you for some of the rules of language . . . you may not be able to state them explicitly . . . but there are very definite rules and we all know what they are . . . the only time problems come in is when you know Chinese or Korean rules and I know American rules and we don't ▓▓▓▓▓▓▓ . . . then we have ▓▓▓▓▓▓▓▓▓▓▓ and lack of communication . . . we don't ▓▓▓▓▓▓▓▓▓ . . . for example . . . if you know football and you try to play with the rules of a soccer game . . . of course ▓▓▓▓▓▓▓▓▓▓▓ . . . you're not going to be able to accomplish what you want to accomplish . . . so in terms of the sociolinguistic way of looking at language . . . language is a kind of rule-governed behavior . . . of interaction between people . . . like a ▓▓▓▓▓▓ . . . everybody knows the ▓▓▓▓▓▓ . . . they're mutually intelligible . . . we all know within a given community . . . ▓▓▓▓▓▓ knows how to play . . . . even if we cannot explicitly state the rules . . . now the big question for you probably and for me if we're trying to learn a language . . . how can I learn the rules of the other language? . . . so part of the definition . . . we can say . . . a rule-governed social behavior . . . is one way of looking at language from a sociological kind of viewpoint.

The lecturer suggests a number of ways that language is like a game. What are they?

Example

You usually need more than one person to "play."

a. _____

b. _____

c. _____

d. _____

e. _____

LISTENING AND NOTE-TAKING STRATEGY

If you do not understand some words or ideas, you can still often get the general idea from the context. If you think an idea might be important, put a question mark (?) in your notes and check with a classmate or the professor later.

F Predicting Content and Lecture Direction

Predicting content and lecture direction helps you to organize your notes in advance and listen more selectively and efficiently. Predicting does not mean knowing the correct answer; it means **making an educated guess**.

Exercise 6

The purpose of this exercise is to demonstrate that you can predict content and lecture direction. The following excerpt is from another linguistics lecture. At thirteen different points, you will be directed to stop listening and reading and discuss with the class what you predict will come next.

Cover each section of the lecture until you are ready to listen to it. Do not read ahead until you have stopped and made a prediction.

What I'd like to do is talk a little about something called nu shu . . . *now has anybody heard of this? . . . it came to scholars' attention primarily in the last few decades even though it's been around for centuries . . . and in the last few years it became very popularly known because there was a book called* Snow Flower and the Secret Fan *written by a woman named Lisa See . . . I don't know if anyone has read it . . . but that really brought* nu shu *to a public light. . . . Anyway . . . anyone? . . .*

Stop and predict

well nu shu *is Chinese for "women's writing" . . . and it's a writing system that was known and used* <u>only</u> *by women . . . and Chinese scholars think it might be the only one of its kind actually in existence . . . and right now fewer than ten people can fluently read or write it and that number is going down every day because the users of* nu shu *are so so old. . . . Okay so let's talk about* nu shu *. . . where is it from . . . when did it start . . .*

Stop and predict

um . . . it has existed as I said for centuries but it has only received scholarly attention in the last few decades . . . and its origins are very obscure . . . nobody really is exactly sure when it came about . . . some scholars say that the script reaches back as far as the third century in a remote part of south-central China . . . others

Stop and predict

have talked about . . . maybe this is a romantic story . . . tracing it back to a concubine of an Emperor about a thousand years ago . . . who, after she went to the court, wanted to communicate with sisters and friends who lived outside of the court . . . okay . . . probably more important than <u>when</u> *is*

Stop and predict

why . . . why was this language created? and if any of you know anything about Chinese history in the past only men learned to read and write Chinese . . . and women's freedom was limited both physically and socially . . . physically women's feet were bound so their mobility truly was limited . . . but also

Stop and predict

socially . . . socially women often had to leave their family and friends when they married . . . moving to other regions . . . so being isolated from friends, from family . . . and it's believed that nu shu *was born as a way for women to communicate with each other . . . to maintain childhood friendships . . . to communicate with female family members even over great distance . . . and so the script over years was passed down from generation to generation, friend to friend, grandmother to granddaughter, and never shared with men and boys . . . and this script allowed the women to express themselves*

4. What are the steps to process and produce black tea?

_____

_____

5. The Designer Food Program of the National Institute of Health is researching forty foods that have unusually powerful disease-fighting abilities. What does it hope to do with this information?

_____

_____

ACTIVITY 11 **COMPARING IDEAS**

1. In small groups, compare your answers to the preceding questions. If you have different answers, check your notes and discuss your reasons for making your choices.

2. Compare your rewritten notes to the sample rewritten notes in Appendix D. Notice the organization. Is yours similar or different? Are your notes equally effective in making important ideas stand out?

ACTIVITY 12 **ACADEMIC WORD LIST VOCABULARY**

Match the word and its meaning. Write the correct letter in the space provided. An example is given to help you see the word in context.

Group 1
a. an idea or issue that one should consider
b. the way parts are put together or organized
c. a group working toward the same goal
d. the steps or method of doing something
e. two-way communication through words, looks, or action
f. frequency of something happening

____ 1. *interaction*   We watched the children's friendly interaction in the playground.

____ 2. *factor*   What factors do we need to think about when studying "quality of life"?

____ 3. *incidence*   The incidence of crime in that neighborhood has gone down.

____ 4. *process*   I jumped at the chance to watch the artist paint; I'd never seen the process from start to end.

____ 5. *structure*   There are three levels of management in the structure of the organization.

____ 6. *team*   They worked together as a team to find a solution.

Group 2
- **a.** to create; to plan
- **b.** to use, eat, drink
- **c.** to separate from others; cause to be alone
- **d.** to limit, restrain, or make an action or behavior difficult
- **e.** to leave unprotected
- **f.** to point to a fact

_____ 7. *consume*   How much chocolate do Americans consume in a year?

_____ 8. *design*   He designed the building with young families' needs in mind.

_____ 9. *expose*   Because the rug had been exposed to sunlight for many years, it had lost its original bright color.

_____ 10. *indicate*   The thermometer indicated that the temperatures were below freezing.

_____ 11. *inhibit*   Very cold temperatures inhibit the growth of bacteria.

_____ 12. *isolate*   Scientists are trying to isolate the genes that carry certain diseases.

ACTIVITY 13 **USING VOCABULARY**

You will hear vocabulary from the lecture and discussion in different contexts. After listening to each item, check (✓) the letter of the closest paraphrase of the information that you heard.

1. _____ **a.** In many countries, people are living longer because they are losing weight.

   _____ **b.** In many countries, people are living longer because they are eating healthier food.

   _____ **c.** In many countries, more and more people expect to improve their eating habits.

2. _____ **a.** The doctor irons all of her clothes for work.

   _____ **b.** The doctor's professional rates are very high.

   _____ **c.** The doctor is respected for her work.

3. _____ **a.** People can take as many vitamins as they want without negative side effects.

   _____ **b.** It is possible to suffer negative side effects from vitamins if taken in high doses.

   _____ **c.** Vitamins rarely work unless taken in great quantities.

4. ___ a. The factory is respected for its work in improving the environment.

___ b. The factory is emitting cancer-causing substances into the environment.

___ c. The factory produces respected drugs that are known to reduce the incidence of cancer.

5. ___ a. In the Pacific, there is an island that is very distant from other places and has a very quickly growing birth rate.

___ b. In the Pacific, there is an island that is very distant from other places and has an unusually high number of babies born with health problems.

___ c. In the Pacific, there is a group of islands where few babies are being born.

ACTIVITY 14 **RETAINING VOCABULARY**

Review the words associated with different body parts. Test your memory of the words by working with a partner and taking turns directing the other to follow a direction involving that body part (e.g., "Point to your heart," "Place your palms face down on the table").

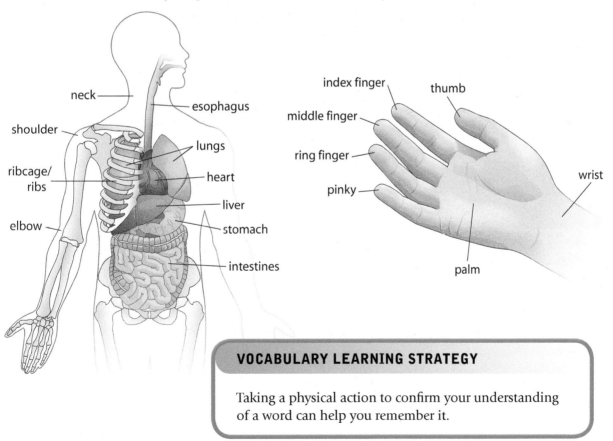

VOCABULARY LEARNING STRATEGY

Taking a physical action to confirm your understanding of a word can help you remember it.

ACTIVITY **15** **BEYOND THE LECTURE: RESEARCHING, SUMMARIZING, WRITING, PUBLISHING**

Complete the following assignment.

Read an article from the library or the Internet about a food, herb, or vitamin and its reported health benefits. Summarize the key points of the article in a paragraph. Publish your findings in a class newsletter with an eye-catching title. Be sure to include references to the original article.

Example

Garlic: Is Grandma Wrong?

The article reported on a study that looked at the health benefits of garlic. During the study, one-half of the participants ate the equivalent of an average clove of garlic in raw form or pill form six days a week for six months. The other half ate a placebo.[1] The study found that regular use of this level of garlic had no effect on cholesterol levels (though bad breath and body odor were reported by more than half the raw garlic eaters). Christopher Gardner of Stanford University in California, the main researcher, was disappointed in the results but said that it is still possible that garlic might improve cholesterol "when eaten in bigger doses or by people with more severe cholesterol problems." He also added that garlic might have other characteristics that might be good for the heart.

Reference
Tanner, L. "Garlic's Health Benefits Minimized." *The Boston Globe* 27 Feb. 2007:A6/ http://www.boston.com/news/nation/articles/2007/02/27/garlics_health_benefits_minimized/.

[1] *placebo:* a substance that looks like real medicine but has no real effects; used in studies for comparison

TYING IT TOGETHER: END-OF-COURSE EVALUATION

Goals

- Synthesize note-taking skills learned in previous units
- Evaluate listening comprehension, note-taking skills, and inferencing skills through quizzes consisting of true/false, multiple-choice, and short-answer questions
- Evaluate application of listening comprehension and note-taking skills through extended written responses incorporating lecture information

DISCUSSION

Listening and Note-Taking Self-Evaluation

1. In your class and throughout this book, you have studied and practiced specific skills and strategies for listening and note-taking. Talk about the skills and strategies that have been most helpful for you.

2. In what ways has your listening and note-taking improved?

3. What do you still find challenging about listening and note-taking?

4. What plans do you have for registering for classes in which you will use the listening and note-taking skills that you have been practicing?

Voter Turnout in the United States (Political Science)

Vocabulary

Related to Voting and Voter Turnout

Check (✓) the words you know. Underline the words you want to learn. Then check their meaning with your instructor or in a dictionary.

candidate
nominee
nominate

party

primary
campaign
party platform

ballot
absentee ballot

cast a ballot
go to the polls

voting booth
polling place

run for office
in the running

drop out of the race

apathy
alienation
disillusionment
mistrust

ACTIVITY **1** **PRE-LECTURE DISCUSSION**

Discuss the charts in small groups. Then answer the questions that follow.

1. This chart reports participation in presidential elections from 1992 to 2004. Using these statistics, draw conclusions about trends in voting and not voting.

Percentage of Voting Age Citizen Population Who Reported Registering or Voting in U.S. Presidential Elections, 1992 to 2008

PRESIDENTIAL ELECTION YEAR[1]	% OF PEOPLE REPORTING THEY REGISTERED	% OF PEOPLE REPORTING THEY VOTED
1992	75.0	68.0
1996	70.9	58.4
2000	69.5	59.5
2004	72.1	63.8
2008	71.0	63.6

Sources: U.S. Bureau of the Census Reports: "Voting and Registration in the Election of November 2004" and http://elections.gmu.edu/CPS_2008.html.

Group's conclusions:

_____

_____

_____

[1] W.J. Clinton won the election in 1992 and 1996. G.W. Bush won in 2000 and 2004. B.H. Obama won in 2008.

2. Look at the following chart reporting participation in the 2004 American presidential election. Percentages are listed according to sex, racial and ethnic group, education, and age. Using these statistics, draw conclusions about tendencies of groups to register, vote, and not vote.

**Reported Rates of Voting and Registration for Citizens
Age 18 Years and Older: 2004**

CHARACTERISTICS	% OF PEOPLE REPORTING THEY REGISTERED	% OF PEOPLE REPORTING THEY VOTED
Total	72.1	63.8
Sex		
Female	73.6	65.4
Male	70.5	62.1
Race and Ethnicity		
White	73.6	65.4
Black	68.7	60.0
Hispanic (of any race)	57.9	47.2
Asian	51.8	44.1
Education		
Higher than a bachelor's degree	87.3	84.2
Bachelor's degree	82.1	77.5
Some college or associate's degree	76.9	68.9
High school graduate or equivalent	66.2	56.4
Less than high school	52.9	39.5
Age		
55 years and older	79.1	71.8
45 to 54 years old	75.5	68.7
35 to 44 years old	72.1	64.0
25 to 34 years old	66.0	55.7
18 to 24 years old	57.6	46.7

Source: U.S. Bureau of the Census, "Voting and Registration in the Election of November 2004."

Group's conclusions:

_____

_____

_____

_____

_____

_____

3. Discuss your answers to the following questions.

   a. Are you surprised by the conclusions you can draw from these statistics? Why or why not?

   b. Why do you think the number of people who report that they register and vote is higher than the number of people who actually do vote?

   c. Why do you think certain groups in the United States have voted less frequently than others?

   d. Why do you think less than two-thirds of the U.S. population as a whole reported voting in the 2004 presidential election? Do you consider this a high, low, or moderate percentage?

   e. In some countries, all citizens are required to vote (and pay a fine if they don't). Do you think this is a good idea? Why or why not?

   f. Do you vote regularly? If so, why? If not, why not?

   g. In 2008, Barack Obama, an African-American man in his 40s, was elected President. During his campaign, there was a noticeable increase in enthusiasm and election participation among younger people and African-Americans. Why, in your opinion?

ACTIVITY 2 **PREPARING FOR THE LECTURE**

The title of the lecture is "Voter Turnout in the United States." What do you expect the lecturer to tell you about this topic? Brainstorm ideas with your classmates.

ACTIVITY 3 **LISTENING FOR THE LARGER PICTURE**

Read the following summary before the lecture begins. Then, listen to the lecture once without taking notes. While listening, fill in the blanks.

1. The lecturer introduces the topic by providing background information about the history of _____ in the United States.

2. The lecturer focuses on the causes of _____.

3. The lecturer classifies _____ into two types: _____ and _____. Then, the lecturer gives examples of each of these types.

4. The lecturer lists the results of a poll asking why _____ and lists the characteristics of voters and nonvoters.

5. Based on this study and others, the lecturer states that a general trend seems to have been that the _____, _____, and _____ have been

underrepresented in the voting booth and that this pattern has not been accidental.

6. The lecturer concludes by giving reasons why the picture is not as bleak as it first appears—because _____

and _____.

7. The lecturer also ends by showing some optimism about the future because

_____.

ACTIVITY 4 DEFINING VOCABULARY

The following words and expressions were used in the lecture that you just heard. You may remember the contexts in which you heard them.

You will hear an additional example of each word or expression in a new context. After listening, check (✓) the letter of the definition that most closely matches what the word or expression means.

1. *eligible*
   ____ a. easy to see
   ____ b. needy; poor
   ____ c. qualified

2. *struggle*
   ____ a. an activity requiring much effort and energy
   ____ b. a game that children play
   ____ c. an activity that gives much pleasure and benefits

3. *apathy*
   ____ a. activity
   ____ b. caring and deep emotion
   ____ c. not caring; indifference

4. *procedure**
   ____ a. steps to do something
   ____ b. problem areas; things to avoid
   ____ c. an illness

5. *deadline*
   ____ a. an illness
   ____ b. a bill
   ____ c. a due date

(continued on next page)

6. *income**

    ____ **a.** money going out; expenditures

    ____ **b.** money coming in; salary

    ____ **c.** educational degrees

7. *time-consuming*

    ____ **a.** taking a little time

    ____ **b.** taking a lot of time

    ____ **c.** taking no time at all

8. *obstacle*

    ____ **a.** an organization that encourages women to achieve their goals

    ____ **b.** a support; something that enables progress

    ____ **c.** a block; something that gets in the way and stops progress

9. *explicit*

    ____ **a.** unclear; imprecise

    ____ **b.** unusual; strange

    ____ **c.** precise; clear

10. *respondent*

    ____ **a.** a person who does something again and again

    ____ **b.** a person who answers a survey

    ____ **c.** a person who conducts a survey

11. *likelihood*

    ____ **a.** probability

    ____ **b.** enjoyability

    ____ **c.** neighborly relations

12. *regardless of (something)*

    ____ **a.** reducing the amount of (something)

    ____ **b.** considering (something) as important

    ____ **c.** without considering (something)

13. *resident**

    ____ **a.** someone who robs a place

    ____ **b.** someone who visits a place

    ____ **c.** someone who lives in a place

14. *status**

    ____ **a.** position in society in terms of importance

    ____ **b.** geographic location; region

    ____ **c.** statistics or numbers

15. *versus*

___ a. in contrast to

___ b. in addition to

___ c. without considering

16. *trend**

___ a. a form of transportation

___ b. a pattern

___ c. an excuse

17. *discourage*

___ a. to spend a lot of money on

___ b. to support; to give strength

___ c. to advise against; to try to prevent

18. *minority*

___ a. a smaller group differing (e.g., in race or religion) from the larger group

___ b. a larger group differing (e.g., in race or religion) from the smaller group

___ c. a group or an organization made up of younger people

19. *optimistic*

___ a. not caring about other people or results

___ b. looking on the negative side

___ c. looking on the positive side

20. *bleak*

___ a. positive

___ b. hopeless

___ c. artistic

ACTIVITY 5 **LISTENING & NOTE-TAKING**

Listen to the lecture a second time and take notes. When you finish, review and revise your notes. Add information that you remember. Consider rewriting your notes. Make the relationship between ideas clear and make important ideas stand out. Hand in your notes to your instructor.

In about a week, your teacher will return your notes and give you a quiz on the information in the lecture. The purpose of this activity is to find out how well your notes help you to retain information.

Discuss the following in small groups.

1. Refer to the conclusions that your group drew from the charts on pages 170 and 171. Did the lecture confirm your conclusions? What voting trends do you expect in the future? Why?

2. Some political scientists and mathematicians blame the low voter turnout on the U.S. election system. Read the article. Then discuss your answers to the questions that follow.

Vetoing[1] the Way America Votes

K.C. COLE, *Los Angeles Times*

Blame electoral woes[2] on how we pick our leaders, mathematicians say. Dumping[3] winner-take-all pluralities[4] could ease apathy, extremism[5] and mudslinging,[6] they add.

Negative campaigning, low voter turnout, elections polarized[7] by such issues as race and abortion—such all-too-familiar ills appear more and more frequently as blotches[8] on the face of American democracy.

But a widely overlooked factor in the elections equation—the mathematics of voting itself—could have the power to at least alleviate,[9] if not cure, these ills, according to political scientists and mathematicians.

In a country where people vote on just about everything—from presidents to prom queens—remarkably little attention is paid to the underlying rules of voting. Most Americans take for granted[10] that the "winner takes all"

system used in most U.S. elections is sacred.[11] People assume that as long as the process of voting is fair, the outcome will represent the wishes of most people, most of the time.

Mathematicians know differently. In fact, for more than 200 years, they have been studying the flaws[12] of voting systems and arguing about which is the least harmful. The subject is well known in academic circles. In 1951, economist Kenneth Arrow proved mathematically that no democratic voting system can be completely fair (and won the Nobel prize for his efforts). This notion is known as "Arrow's impossibility theorem" because it proves that perfect democracy is impossible.

"Every system has something wrong with it," said Temple University mathematician John Allen Paulos, "but some work better more often." Mathematicians do not agree on the best system. But they have no problem

---

[1] *veto:* to say "no" to something
[2] *woes:* complaints, problems
[3] *dump:* to get rid of; to eliminate
[4] *plurality:* majority
[5] *extremism:* lack of moderation
[6] *mudsling:* to say bad and unfair things about someone else
[7] *polarize:* to push to opposing views
[8] *blotch:* a spot or ugly stain
[9] *alleviate:* to relieve; to make less hurtful or difficult
[10] *take for granted:* to believe to be true without thought

[11] *sacred:* holy; so special that it should not be harmed or changed in any way
[12] *flaw:* imperfection; failure

pointing their fingers at the worst: the plurality system used in most U.S. elections.

The issue is of more than academic interest. Plurality systems hand victory[13] to the candidate with the most votes even if that candidate falls far short of a majority and even if the candidate is the person the majority likes least. The current systems can encourage extremism, reward name-calling, alienate[14] voters, and fail to reflect the wishes of most of the people much of the time.

The experts disagree about which alternative system is best. Some, for example, argue for approval voting, which allows everyone to cast one vote per candidate—changing the "one person, one vote" system to "one candidate, one vote." The candidate thus "approved of" by the most voters wins. While plurality systems encourage candidates to take extreme positions that develop a hard core of support, approval voting requires candidates to appeal[15] for broad support. The system, experts believe, might do a lot to eliminate negative campaigning. "You would want to get at least partial approval from supporters of your opposition," Steven Brams, political scientist and mathematician, said. Approval voting would also help minority candidates. "Minorities can't be ignored because majority candidates need their support to win."

Approval voting is not without its detractors,[16] however. Paulos argues that it tends to produce bland,[17] mediocre[18] winners. "Someone who doesn't have any sharp

edges won't turn people off," he said. "But sometimes you want someone who polarizes people because one of the poles is right."

The system Paulos likes much better is cumulative[19] voting, in which voters can give several votes to a single candidate they feel strongly about. As in approval voting, each voter has as many votes as candidates and can distribute[20] those votes among the candidates or give them all to one candidate. "It's a good way to give minorities a voice," said Paulos. "Any group that has sufficient cohesion[21] to vote as a bloc can win."

Robert Richie, the director of the Center for Voting and Democracy, favors a system called preference voting—also known as the transferable ballot. Under preference voting, each voter ranks each candidate first, second, third, and so forth. But if after an initial count, someone's first-place choice seems doomed[22] to defeat,[23] then that voter's second-place vote is counted instead. While preference voting may sound complicated, Richie said it is used in other countries without problems and generates far better voter turnouts than in the U.S. "It's not any harder than learning the rules of baseball or basketball," Richie said.

In the end, deciding on the fairest voting system will probably come down to, well, voting. "Before you decide on the substance, you have to decide what voting method you're going to use," said Paulos. "And then, what method are we going to use to choose the method? It can get all tangled[24] and awful."

---

[13] **victory:** winning
[14] **alienate:** to make someone feel separate or unincluded
[15] **appeal:** to ask (for help)
[16] **detractor:** critic (opposite of supporter)
[17] **bland:** mild, boring; having few outstanding characteristics
[18] **mediocre:** average

[19] **cumulative:** adding amounts together over time
[20] **distribute:** to divide and spread
[21] **cohesion:** sticking together
[22] **doomed:** certain to reach a bad end
[23] **defeat:** failure to win
[24] **tangled:** confused and complicated

a. How many different types of voting systems are mentioned in the article? What are they? How do they work?

b. Which system is generally used in the United States? According to the article, what problems are associated with it?

c. What voting systems are used in countries with which you are familiar? What are the pros and cons of those systems?

ACTIVITY 7 USING YOUR NOTES TO PREPARE FOR THE QUIZ

STUDY STRATEGY

Prepare yourself for tests by predicting questions (short-answer, true/false, multiple-choice, fill-in-the-blank, essay) that you expect the professor to ask. Review with classmates, taking turns asking and answering these questions.

Did you know?

The U.S. Presidential election of 1876 had the highest voter turnout, with 81.8% of eligible voters participating.

Write five questions that you think the professor might ask on the quiz.

1. _____

2. _____

3. _____

4. _____

5. _____

ACTIVITY 8 BEYOND THE LECTURE: WRITING A LETTER TO A NEWSPAPER

Complete the assignment.

The *Los Angeles Times* article on page 176 suggests that the system of voting used in the United States, the "winner takes all" system, has some serious drawbacks. The article mentions other systems and their pros and cons. Based on your experience and knowledge, which of the author's points do you agree with? Which do you disagree with? Write an e-mail to the editor in response to the article.

From: ....   To: L.A. Times Editor
Sent: ....
Subject: RE: Vetoing the Way America Votes

I just finished reading K.C. Cole's article on different voting systems and I thought I'd share my perspective as someone who comes from another country ....

....

....

....

....

LECTURE 12

The Pyramids of Egypt: An Engineering Feat

(Engineering/History)

Vocabulary

Related to Engineering and Construction

Check (✓) the words you know. Underline the words you want to learn. Then check their meaning with your instructor or in a dictionary.

site
foundation
base

survey

mortar
concrete
cement
plywood
lumber
brick

crane
bulldozer

*mason/stonemason/
    masonry*
bricklayer
carpenter/carpentry
surveyor
architect/architecture

blueprint
architectural plan

ACTIVITY **1** **PRE-LECTURE READING AND DISCUSSION**

Discuss your answers to the following in small groups.

1. What monuments are pictured above? What do you know about their construction and purpose?

2. Read the article on the next page about a recent archaeological find in Egypt. Then answer the questions that follow.

World's Oldest Paved Road Found in Egypt

THOMAS H. MAUGH II, *Los Angeles Times*

American researchers have discovered the world's oldest paved road, a 4,600-year-old highway that linked[1] a quarry[2] in a desolate[3] region of the Egyptian desert to waterways that carried blocks to monument[4] sites along the Nile.

The eight-mile road is at least 500 years older than any previously discovered road and is the only paved road discovered in ancient Egypt, said geologist Thomas Bown of the United States Geological Survey in Denver, who reported the discovery Friday.

"The road probably doesn't rank with the pyramids as a construction feat,[5] but it is a major engineering achievement," said his colleague, geologist James Harrell of the University of Toledo. "Not only is the road earlier than we thought possible, we didn't even think they built roads."

The researchers made an additional discovery in the quarry at the northern end of the road: the first evidence that the Egyptians used rock saws.[6] "This is the oldest example of saws being used for cutting stone," said archaeologist James K. Hoffmeier of Wheaton College in Illinois.

"That's two technologies we didn't know they had," Harrell said. "And we don't know why they were both abandoned."[7]

The road was discovered in the Faiyum Depression about 45 miles southwest of Cairo. Short segments of the road had been observed by earlier explorers, Bown said, but they failed to realize its significance or follow up on their observations. The road was clearly built to service the newly discovered quarry. Bown and Harrell have found the camp that housed workers at the quarry, and numerous artifacts[8] date the site to the Egyptian Old Kingdom that began about 2600 B.C.

The road appears today to go nowhere, ending in the middle of the desert. When it was built, its terminus[9] was a quay[10] on the shore of Lake Moeris, which had an elevation of about 66 feet above sea level, the same as the quay. Birket Qarun, the lake that is now at the bottom of the depression, has a surface elevation of 148 feet below sea level, reflecting the sharp change in climate in the region.

Lake Moeris received its water from the annual floods of the Nile. At the time of the floods, the river and lake were at the same level and connected through a gap[11] in the hills near the modern villages of el-Lahun and Hawara. Harrell and Bown believe that blocks were loaded onto barges[12] during the dry season, then floated over to the Nile during the floods[13] to be shipped off to the monument sites at Giza and Saqqara.

---

[1] **link:** to connect
[2] **quarry:** a place to mine rocks and stones
[3] **desolate:** empty of people
[4] **monument:** a statue (or building) built in memory of someone or an event
[5] **feat:** an impressive act
[6] **saw:** a tool with a handle and a sharp, rough edge usually used for cutting wood or metal
[7] **abandon:** to discontinue or leave forever

[8] **artifact:** an object used in ancient times
[9] **terminus:** endpoint
[10] **quay:** a place to exit or unload ships
[11] **gap:** empty space
[12] **barge:** a long boat for carrying heavy loads
[13] **flood:** an overflow of water

Now answer the following questions.

   a. What discoveries are mentioned in the article?

   b. "The road appears today to go nowhere." Did it really go nowhere? What was the road used for?

   c. Why is the discovery important?

ACTIVITY **2** **PREPARING FOR THE LECTURE**

The title of the lecture is "The Pyramids of Egypt: An Engineering Feat." What do you expect the lecturer to tell you? Brainstorm ideas with your classmates.

ACTIVITY **3** **LISTENING FOR THE LARGER PICTURE**

Read the following questions. Then, listen to the lecture once without taking notes. After listening, answer the questions.

   1. Which of the following does the lecturer do? Check (✓) more than one.

      ____ **a.** Speaks about the daily life of the ancient Egyptians

      ____ **b.** Speaks about the lives and accomplishments of different ancient Egyptian kings

      ____ **c.** Provides information about when the Egyptian pyramids were constructed

      ____ **d.** Compares and contrasts pyramids built in Egypt to those built in Mexico

      ____ **e.** Gives details to describe one pyramid in particular, the Great Pyramid of Khufu in Giza

      ____ **f.** Describes the three types of pyramids found in Egypt

      ____ **g.** Explains the process required to build the pyramid

   2. Why were the Egyptian pyramids built?

      _____

      _____

Did you know?

The Great Pyramid at Giza in Egypt, constructed around 2500 B.C.E., was the tallest building in the world until the Eiffel Tower was erected in 1889.

The following words and expressions were used in the lecture that you just heard. You may remember the contexts in which you heard them.

🎧 **You will hear an additional example of each word or expression in a new context. After listening, check (✓) the letter of the definition that most closely matches what you think the word or expression means.**

1. *tomb*

____ **a.** a cemetery

____ **b.** a chamber for the burial of the dead; a monument commemorating the dead

____ **c.** a soldier who died in battle

2. *spirit*

____ **a.** soul; the central quality or force within someone

____ **b.** body; the physical nature of an individual

____ **c.** death; the loss of life

3. *steep slope*

____ **a.** a nearly flat surface, changing only slightly in height or angle

____ **b.** a means of transportation (like a bicycle) for climbing hills

____ **c.** a surface set at a large angle, either rising or falling

4. *progression*

____ **a.** a useful and practical event

____ **b.** a unique and special event, unrelated to others

____ **c.** a series or sequence of related events

5. *symbolic**

____ **a.** representative

____ **b.** beautiful

____ **c.** historic

6. *core**

____ **a.** the imagination; the creativity

____ **b.** the center; the essence

____ **c.** the beauty; the image

7. *level*

____ **a.** smooth, flat, and even

____ **b.** rough and shaky

____ **c.** characterized by ups and downs

8. *soak*

    ____ **a.** to postpone or delay an action

    ____ **b.** to clean to a spotless state

    ____ **c.** to stay in water for a long time

9. *swell*

    ____ **a.** to increase in roundness and fullness

    ____ **b.** to treat an injury with an ice pack or heating pad

    ____ **c.** to fall

10. *drag*

    ____ **a.** to lift above the head in order to carry

    ____ **b.** to request assistance in order to move something

    ____ **c.** to cause to move along the ground

11. *coffin*

    ____ **a.** a box in which a dead person is buried

    ____ **b.** a white sheet in which a dead person is buried

    ____ **c.** a cemetery with separate sections for people of different religions

12. *layer**

    ____ **a.** something sweet and fattening

    ____ **b.** a thickness, often one of many

    ____ **c.** someone who does not tell the truth

13. *ramp*

    ____ **a.** a type of wheelchair used by people with disabilities

    ____ **b.** stairs connecting one level to another

    ____ **c.** a manmade gradual path connecting two different levels

14. *speculate*

    ____ **a.** to think about something without having enough facts to reach a certain conclusion

    ____ **b.** to take sides in divorce proceedings

    ____ **c.** to be certain about something

15. *ponder*

    ____ **a.** to swim in order to get exercise

    ____ **b.** to give advice or suggestions about something

    ____ **c.** to think deeply about something

In addition to these words, the lecturer also uses terms for various hand tools and construction devices and equipment: *wedges, chisels, mallets, saws, hammers, ropes, sledges, wheeled vehicles, levers, cranes, bulldozers.* The lecturer also refers to a specific stone (*limestone*) and certain metals (*gold, copper, iron, bronze*). If you don't know some of these words, check their meaning with your instructor or in a dictionary.

ACTIVITY 5 LISTENING AND NOTE-TAKING

Listen to the lecture a second time and take notes. When you finish, review and revise your notes. Add information that you remember. Consider rewriting your notes. Make the relationship between ideas clear and make important ideas stand out. Hand in your notes to your instructor.

In about a week, your teacher will return your notes and give you a quiz on the information in the lecture. The purpose of this activity is to find out how well your notes help you to retain information.

ACTIVITY 6 POST-LECTURE DISCUSSION

Discuss your answers to the following questions with a small group.

1. The lecturer ends the lecture by saying:

   these pyramids of ancient Egypt allow us glimpses into worlds of long ago . . . and it makes me wonder when I think about them . . . what is our legacy to the future? . . . what legacy are we going to pass down to our descendants? . . . what's going to remain of us and our technological achievements 5,000 years in the future? . . . I think these are questions that are worth pondering . . .

   How would you answer these questions?

2. Imagine that you have been given the job of burying a time capsule for the current year. Everything will be placed in a room-sized box, which is designed to last and protect its contents for 5,000 years. What will you include in that box to give your descendants an accurate idea of life today?

ACTIVITY 7 USING YOUR NOTES TO PREPARE FOR THE QUIZ

STUDY STRATEGIES

1. Remember to prepare yourself for tests by predicting questions (short-answer, true/false, multiple-choice, fill-in-the-blank, essay) that you expect the professor to ask. Review with classmates, taking turns asking and answering these questions.

2. Start reviewing your notes days before the test (or longer, depending on the size of the test). Review regularly and, especially, shortly before the test.

Write five questions that you think the professor might ask on the quiz.

1. _____

2. _____

3. _____

4. _____

5. _____

ACTIVITY 8 **BEYOND THE LECTURE: ESSAY TEST QUESTIONS**

Write an essay on one of the following topics. Successfully answering essay test questions involves paying close attention to responding to *all* parts of the question.

1. In what ways does the significance of the pyramids extend beyond their function as burial places for kings? Use data, facts, and information from the lecture to support your ideas. Consider knowledge that we have gained about the religion, social structure, and technology of ancient Egypt. How might this knowledge be important or have relevance to our lives now?

2. a. Discuss what the pyramids tell us about life in Egypt 5,000 years ago. Use data, facts, and information from the lecture to support your ideas.

   b. What modern technological achievements do you think will be remembered 5,000 years from now? What do you think they will show others about our society?

3. a. Discuss how the culture and environment of ancient Egypt impacted the construction and design of the pyramids. Use data, facts, and information from the lecture to support your ideas.

   b. Choose a location that you know well. Discuss how the culture and environment of that location have impacted the design and construction of its buildings (e.g., houses, shopping malls, churches and temples, office buildings).

The following words come from the Academic Word List (AWL). The numbers in parentheses indicate the lectures where the words are used.

accurate (7)
achievement (5)
acknowledge (5)
adapt (4) (5)
adequately (8)
alternative/alternate (6)
analysis (7)
approximately (3) (6)
assume/assumption (7)
attitude (4)
attribute (6) (9)
aware (4)

benefit (5)

category (8)
commodity (4)
complex (4)
concentrate/concentration (9)
consume/consumption (4) (10)
contribute (6)
core (12)
create/creation (9)

design (10)
despite (4)
detect (8)
diminish (7)
distinct/distinction/distinctive (9)
document (4)
dominate (6)
domination/dominance (9)

enable (8)
energy (6)
enormous (4), enormity (9)
environment (8)
establish (4)
ethnicity (3)
eventually (6)
evolve/evolution (9)
exclusive (8)
expose (10)

factor (10)
finance (4)
focus (3) (7)
function (8)

generate/generation (3) (6)

hierarchy (4)

implication (3)
incidence (10)
income (11)
indicate/indication/indicative (9)
inevitable (5)
inhibit (10)
interact (10)
invest/investment (3)
isolate (10)
item (7)

layer (12)

maintain (8), maintenance (9)
major (7)
mature (3)
method (7)
minimize (5)
minor (4)
monitor (5)
mutually (8)

obviously (8)
occur (5), occurrence (9)

perspective (3)
phenomena (3)
potential (4)
predominant (6)
primarily (8)
process (10)
procedure (11)
prohibit (4)

randomly (3)
range (8)
regionally (3)
relax (4)
release (8)
research (3)
resident (11)
respond/response (5) (8)
reverse (8)

sector (3)
similar (7), similarity (9)
solely (8)
source (6)
specifically (3)
specify/specification/specificity (9)
stable/unstable (7)
statistically (3)
status (11)
structure (10)
sufficient (7)
survey (3)
symbolic (12)

target (4)
team (10)
technique (7)
technology (7)
tradition (8)
transport/transportation (6)
trend (4) (11)

undergo (7)

vary/variation (3) (7) (9)
virtually (5)

The organizational plan indicated occurs in either the entire lecture or a significant part of it.

ORGANIZATIONAL PLAN	LECTURE NUMBER AND TITLE
Defining a Term	**LECTURE 2:** "Nu Shu": Women's Unique Language
	LECTURE 5: How to Deal with Stress
	LECTURE 6: Acid Rain
	LECTURE 8: Pheromones
	LECTURE 9: The Near Side of the Moon
Listing Subtopics	**LECTURE 1:** Study Tips
	LECTURE 2: "Nu Shu": Women's Unique Language
	LECTURE 3: Exploring a Market: Attitudes toward Pets
	LECTURE 4: Tobacco through the Millennia
	LECTURE 5: How to Deal with Stress
	LECTURE 11: Voter Turnout in the United States
Describing a Causal Relationship	**LECTURE 1:** Study Tips
	LECTURE 2: "Nu Shu": Women's Unique Language
	LECTURE 6: Acid Rain
	LECTURE 11: Voter Turnout in the United States
Exemplifying a Topic	**LECTURE 7:** Archaeological Dating Methods
	LECTURE 8: Pheromones
	LECTURE 11: Voter Turnout in the United States
Describing a Process or Sequence of Events	**LECTURE 4:** Tobacco through the Millennia
	LECTURE 7: Archaeological Dating Methods
	LECTURE 10: Drink Your Green Tea!
	LECTURE 12: The Pyramids of Egypt: An Engineering Feat
Classifying Subtopics	**LECTURE 8:** Pheromones
	LECTURE 9: The Near Side of the Moon
	LECTURE 10: Drink Your Green Tea!
	LECTURE 11: Voter Turnout in the United States
	LECTURE 12: The Pyramids of Egypt: An Engineering Feat
Describing Characteristics	**LECTURE 2:** "Nu Shu": Women's Unique Language
	LECTURE 9: The Near Side of the Moon
	LECTURE 12: The Pyramids of Egypt: An Engineering Feat
Comparing and Contrasting	**LECTURE 2:** "Nu Shu": Women's Unique Language
	LECTURE 9: The Near Side of the Moon
	LECTURE 10: Drink Your Green Tea!
	LECTURE 11: Voter Turnout in the United States
Making a Generalization and Providing Evidence	**LECTURE 1:** Study Tips
	LECTURE 10: Drink Your Green Tea!
	LECTURE 11: Voter Turnout in the United States

LECTURE 5 — How to Deal With Stress

What is Stress?

STRESS — term originally used in physics

(to describe force betw. 2 touching masses)

— 40 years ago, Hans Selye adapted term

"the body's nonspecific response (incl. ↑ breathing,

heart rate, blood pressure, muscle tension) to any

demand placed on it, good or bad"

EUSTRESS (stress from good things)   e.g., tests

e.g., vacation, marriage

— Stress not hazardous in itself. Danger is in reaction to stress.

Ways to deal w/stress appropriately:

1. Learn to recognize signals of stress (before out of control)

   e.g., irritability, insomnia, rapid weight loss/gain, ↑ smoking or drinking,

   ↑ "dumb" errors, phys. tension, tics, tightness of breath...

   When see early signs, protect self! (withdraw fr. situation, reward self...)

2. Pay attention to body

   exercise/nutrition can ↓ effect of stress on body & mind

   — provides stress-free environment

3. Make plans & act when approp. (instead of worrying)

4. Learn to accept situations which are out of your control

   (only ↑ stress if try to resist inevitable!)

5. Pace activities

   break task into manageable parts

   start fresh each day — recognize only 24 hrs./day!

Acid rain (AR): "any form of precipitation that contains high levels of acid
(partic. sulfuric acid & nitric acid)"

pH — scale for measuring acidity (7 = neutral)

pure rain = pH 5.6

lowest AR in U.S. = 1.4!

Causes

When N (nitrogen) and S (sulfur) go into atmosphere, they combine
w/ O (oxygen) and H (hydrogen)… form nitric acid (HNO_3) and
sulfuric acid (H_2SO_4)

Nitrogen sources (in U.S. 2002)

54% — transportation

22% — electric utilities

17% — fuel combustion (other purposes)

7% — industrial & other sources

Sulfur sources (in U.S.)

67% — electric util. (mostly coal-burning power plants)

19% — fuel combustion (not for electricity)

9% — other industrial sources

5% — transportation

Effects

On aquatic ecosystems: fish pops. ↓ or disappear

acid water kills fish or prevents reproduction

lakes look healthy but not true

On forests: certain trees die

                                    Why? acidity strips protective surface

                                                    ↓

                                        trees vulnerable to water loss/disease

On architectural   buildings dissolving/crumbling

    structures: billions $/yr. to replace

On health: no direct health effects

                           maybe indirect neg. effects (e.g., illness from
                                leaching of toxic metals in pipes)

Conclusions:

    AR ↑ w/industrialization

        (H_2O in glaciers from 200 yrs. ago (before Indust. Revolution) pH ~5

    What to do? Consider:

        shift to alternative nonpolluting energy

        create tech. to reduce release of S and N

            occurring worldwide

                new pollution-reduction laws (for cars, industry)

                agreements betw. countries to ↓ emissions

                problem: ↑ demand for power, transportation

    AR — problem w/no natl. boundaries!

Archaeological Dating Methods:

Dendrochronology: tree-ring dating
                    one of oldest methods

— measures tree rings which vary w/climatic changes
   (cross section of tree shows concentric rings)
      — pale ring   — spring   — thin ring   — drought or cold spell
      — dark "   — winter   — thick "   — abundant water/sunlight
   — can measure back 1000s of years by matching rings w/known
      climatic events (don't need to count all)

Carbon-14 dating method — all living things contain radioactive C-14
                          isotopes which disintegrate at fixed
element w/same   rate when organism dies ($\frac{1}{2}$ every 5730 yrs.)
# of protons but
diff. # of neutrons   "half-life"
                        point at which half of element diminishes

— scientists use geiger counter to measure C-14 signals fr. old material
   & compare this w/signals from living sample
      e.g., live sample: 75 disintegrations/min.
      old sample: 37.5 disintegrations/min.
      ∴ old sample = 5,730 yrs. old

Drawbacks of C-14 method:
   — requires large sample (up to 10 oz.)
   — destroys sample

Recent advances in C-14 dating: AMS: Accelerated Mass Spectrometry
   — focuses on measuring C-14 atoms rather than electric signals emitted
      by disintegration
   — advantages: smaller samples (1—2 mg.)

C-14 dating is limited to 60,000 yrs.

There are other methods.

Most methods cross-checked for accuracy.

Pheromones —"chemical substance released by organism into environment
          to evoke response from other members of same species"
    — detected by smell or taste
    — widely used by animals — from 1 cell to higher primates
  — Characteristics
    — highly sensitive
    — highly specific (each species responds only to own pheromones;
      no effect on other species)
Types of pheromones:
  primer pher.   — causes phys. change in organism
              — affects development & later behavior
                e.g., queen bee prevents reproductive develop.
                of ♀ worker bees
  releaser pher. — produces rapid & reversible response
              — immed. change
      4 types (not mutually exclusive):
        — alarm pher.
          — warns of danger; response to threat
            e.g., mouse releases odor; causes others to flee
        — aggregation pher.
          — calls members to 1 place for food, shelter, mating, etc.
            e.g., honey bees — odor identifies colony; attracts
            bees to colony
        — sex pher.
          — sexually arouses/attract species
            e.g., mature female snails attract undifferentiated
            snails (neither ♀ nor ♂) & cause it to develop into ♂
        — terrestrial trail pher.
          — navigational guide
            e.g., ants follow trail to food
Pher. important to agriculture
      Why?
        — can control animal behavior to protect crops
        — don't contain poison like traditional insecticides
        — only affect 1 species; won't harm other species

Surface features of near side of moon — side perpetually turned to earth
<u>flat lowlands — maria (pl. "sea") mare (s.)</u> vs. <u>highlands — mountain ranges</u>

 — called "seas" but no liquid water
 — fairly smooth
 — made of valleys & basins filled
   w/molten lava
   — basalt rock (igneous rock)
 — certain maria — areas of high
   concentration of mass (mascon)
   — mascon exert increased
     gravitational pull on
     spacecraft overhead
 — circular maria (assoc. w/mascons)
   — up to 702 mi. diameter
 — irreg. maria larger

 — lighter color & brighter than maria
 — dominated by craters
   — craters range in size
     up to 150 mi.
 — highlands extend 100s of miles
   & up to 3.5a mi. above maria

Water on moon?
 — Until recently, scientists said no water on moon because moon lacked
   atmosphere (earth has liquid water because has atmosphere)
 — Now... questions!
   1998 lunar probe sent data showing possibility of ice crystals (in soil) in
   craters at lunar poles
 — if true — very important! ice could provide components for rocket fuel
 — issue needs more research
 — even if true... we don't have technol. to use ice yet!

Temperature on moon?
 — drastic changes in daily temp. — range from 215°F. (102° C) → −285°F. (-176°C)
   Why?   no atmosphere (earth's atmos. is moderating blanket & limits
               diff. betw. day & night)

Light of near side of moon
 — no twilight/dawn
 — darkness/light — immediate when sun goes up or down (except for
   small # of reflections from nearby peaks)
   Why?   lack of atmosphere — nothing reflects light
(moon — 238,600 mi. away)

All tea — fr. camellia sinensis — evergreen, tropical, & semitrop. climates

3 ways to process tea leaves:

Green tea	Black tea	Oolong tea
"virgin" tea — least	more processing	semi-fermented
processed (~3 hr. process)	(needs fermentation)	green-brown
leaves steamed & heated	spread leaves in cool,	
to soften (& stop oxidation)	humid place	
↓	↓	
rolled (to remove	O_2 interacts w/leaves	
moisture)	(oxidation/fermentation)	
	causes leaves → black	
	↓	
↓	hot, dry air (15–25 min.)	
dried	stops oxidation	

World production: 20%   75%   4%

<u>Green tea is good for you!</u>

— Studies in China: G.T. reduces # of cancer esophagus

— Studies (Japan)   ↓ lung cancer among people drinking GT

↓ stomach cancer

↓ skin tumors

↓ blood cholesterol

— GT contains vit. C

— av. 2 cups GT = 1 cup OJ

— U.S. study — GT may help protect against cavities

Continuing research GT?

— studied in NIH program w/40 other disease-fighting foods

e.g., garlic, carrots

— scientists want to isolate & synthesize disease-fighting element

Why? preventative medicine

Problem? what element?

— focusing on "polyphenols"

GT — no known toxicity... won't hurt... may help

mild stimulant... GT < caffeine than coffee, black tea, soda

free from restrictions of the time . . . and words were hidden in notes, fans, weaving, embroidery . . . and one of the most famous examples of how it was used . . . the one that's actually being looked at a lot nowadays . . . is . . . there was something called a Third Day Book . . .

Stop and predict

and the story behind these books is they were kinds of journals or diaries . . . and when a girl would get married and she'd be going to another place to live she would receive from her closest girlfriends and from her mother a book with messages and wishes for her in this marriage . . . but most of the book was empty . . . the pages were empty, . . . and in this book the bride would spend the rest of her life recording her experiences throughout her married life . . . and so these books—written in nu shu *so they couldn't be understood by men or boys—are actually wonderful sources of information about the thoughts and the lives of these women . . . now many of these books aren't around anymore because*

Stop and predict

they were so precious to the women that often they had them buried or burned with them when they died so that they could make sure that their thoughts stayed private into the next world . . . amazing documents . . . so . . . so . . . what are the characteristics of nu shu *that make it different from written Chinese? What does it look like? . . .*

Stop and predict

well <u>like</u> Chinese, it's written from top to bottom in columns and then read from right to left . . . but there are a number of key differences . . .

Stop and predict

for one thing, as you might know written Chinese is made up of characters . . . ideograms we might call them . . . which represent <u>ideas</u> not sounds . . . nu shu *on the other hand contains letters which represent <u>sounds</u> . . . it's a phonetic type of writing . . .*

Stop and predict

and it looks different from Chinese . . . in some ways it looks like a Chinese in which characters were stretched and altered . . . it's more delicate than Chinese . . . and the characters have been described as wispy and elongated . . . and finally, another thing is that experts estimate that the language has between 1,800 and 2,500 characters each representing a syllable of the local dialect . . . in contrast to Mandarin Chinese which has 30,000 ideograms each with a different meaning . . . so clearly it's not as complex as Mandarin . . . as Chinese itself . . . but it was certainly useful . . . okay what's the situation of nu shu *now? . . .*

Stop and predict

now there's really no reason for young girls anymore to learn nu shu *as a form of communication because they're learning Chinese reading and writing along with the boys . . . but scholars are interested in these Third Day books and embroideries and other things that have survived that offer such a unique perspective into the lives and thoughts of people who didn't have a very public voice . . . and so they're compiling dictionaries of* nu shu *to understand its structure and the women who used it . . . and finally there is actually . . . interestingly enough . . . there are* <u>commercial</u> *interests in recent years. . .*

Stop and predict

recently, a foundation donated a couple of hundred thousand dollars to build a museum to preserve the remaining Third Day books and embroidered nu shu *. . . and a Hong Kong company has invested several million yuan for the construction of roads hotels and parks all aimed at exploiting* nu shu's *growing fame in this remote area in China . . . and what's happening in this village where a lot of this activity is centered—where a lot of the* nu shu *activity was centered—is that it's changed some of the relationships between the sexes in a way that would have really shocked the writers of the old Third Day books because*

Stop and predict

now that the women there are actually bringing in some money through nu shu *. . . researchers are going there . . . even tourists are going there . . . women have actually moved to the center of this community's economic and cultural life and so the fact that people are coming to hear the women sing and sew and write . . . this has brought them a little bit of power . . . an interesting result of a language that in some ways was born out of powerlessness and was a way to reclaim power.*

How did you do? Were you able to predict the direction of the lecture at least some of the time? If so, that's good. Once again, predicting does not mean knowing the right answer; it means making an educated guess.

LISTENING AND NOTE-TAKING STRATEGY

Cues to organization and topic introductions help you predict what the lecturer is going to talk about. The more you can predict, the more you can understand and note because you are ready for what is ahead. Also, predicting keeps you alert and focused and an active rather than a passive listener.

RECOGNIZING INTRODUCTIONS, CONCLUSIONS, AND DIGRESSIONS

DISCUSSION

Your Preferences and Expectations of Professors

Goals

- Recognize introductions, conclusions, and digressions
- Use introductions to predict a lecturer's direction and goals
- Use conclusions to confirm understanding of key points

1. Think about your past experiences listening to lecturers (in English or in another language). What can you remember about the lecturers who were the most enjoyable? least enjoyable? easiest to follow? most difficult to follow?

2. Which professor would you choose if you were taking a course in your native language in your major? What if you were taking the course in English?
   - **Professor A:** entertaining; interesting; knowledgeable; somewhat disorganized; digresses a lot while lecturing, which makes it sometimes difficult to follow; fair grader
   - **Professor B:** monotonous voice and dull presentation; very knowledgeable; very organized; easy grader
   - **Professor C:** entertaining; interesting; knowledgeable; organized; very demanding in terms of homework; gives very few As

A Using Introductions to Recognize Lecture Focus and Direction

Lecturers start their lectures in different ways. For example, a lecturer could do one or more of the following:

- begin with some sort of introductory remarks and cues
- provide background information that leads up to the topic
- begin with a few personal stories or comments about a shared experience to relax the audience
- review or summarize previously learned material before talking about that day's focus
- give an overview of the whole lecture plan and explicitly state the lecture goals
- give general statements about a topic

Listeners need to recognize when the speaker finishes the introduction and begins the body of the lecture, which contains the key points.

LISTENING AND NOTE-TAKING STRATEGY

Most often, the introduction is a good time for listeners to *listen* (rather than rush to note) in order to get a clear idea about the lecturer's goals for the lecture. This way, listeners have a framework or plan for predicting what will be discussed in the lecture and can later check to see if their notes, in fact, reflect those goals.

CUES TO RECOGNIZE INTRODUCTIONS

1. Sentences that give an overview of the lecturer's specific goals:

   I'd like to do two things. The first is to define X. The second is to give a few examples of X.

   I'm going to start out with a few slides, and the point is to show you . . .

2. Sentences that indicate a lecture's general focus:

   We're going to be talking about X today.

   (So) let's talk about X . . .

3. Sentences or rhetorical questions that refer to a continuation of a previous lecture:

   Last time we were talking about X.

   Where did we leave off yesterday?

Exercise

 You will hear the beginnings of five different lectures. First, read the question about each excerpt. Then listen to the excerpt. After listening, check (✓) the best answer.

Example

This sociology lecture will be about

_____ a. the physical and emotional benefits and drawbacks of being an employed woman or a housewife

_____ b. the reactions of the world to employed women and housewives

_____ c. the effects of the women's liberation movement

_____ d. the working habits of women in the United States

The lecturer said:

What I would like to focus on in this lecture are some of the factors a woman might want to take into account when deciding whether to enter the job market or not. . . . A major question would be which one is emotionally and physically more beneficial. . . .

Other ideas were mentioned in the introduction, but this statement addresses the focus of the lecture. It indicates that the body of the lecture will be about the physical and emotional benefits and drawbacks of being an employed woman or a housewife. Therefore, the best answer is (a).

1. This psychology lecture will be about

   _____ a. language

   _____ b. motor skills

   _____ c. stages of child cognitive[1] development

   _____ d. none of the above

2. This health lecture will be about

   _____ a. the many things we eat that are harmful to us

   _____ b. people's attitudes toward new findings about the side effects of certain foods

   _____ c. a study that showed the effect of alcohol on the fetus[2]

   _____ d. the type of foods that pregnant women should not eat

---

[1] *cognitive:* relating to judgment and reasoning
[2] *fetus:* an unborn being (in humans, from the ninth week to birth)

3. This ecology[3] lecture will be about

____ a. the basic structure of all ecosystems[4]

____ b. particular ecosystems and their characteristics

____ c. the differences among ecosystems

____ d. human influences on ecosystems

4. This sociology lecture will be about

____ a. the reasons for American marriage and divorce trends[5]

____ b. American marriage and divorce trends over a period of time

____ c. what non-Americans think of American marriage and divorce trends

____ d. the effects of American marriage and divorce trends

5. This psychology lecture will be about

____ a. how we can help ourselves become happier

____ b. how we can help communities become happier

____ c. how we can help society become happier

____ d. all of the above

B Recognizing and Comprehending Conclusions

Some lecturers end their lectures suddenly. They may say, "Oh! Time's up. I'll continue tomorrow." However, many lecturers use conclusions to finalize their lectures. Conclusions can do one or more of the following:

- review the lecture's key points
- make general statements that connect different aspects of the topic
- discuss the topic's consequences

Conclusions that involve a review or a generalization provide the listeners with a chance to check whether their notes reflect what the lecturer thought was important.

LISTENING AND NOTE-TAKING STRATEGY

If a lecturer gives a conclusion that reviews his or her goals or summarizes an example or story, you have an opportunity to confirm that you have noted the key points.

---

[3] **ecology:** the science that deals with the interrelationships between organisms and their environment
[4] **ecosystem:** a system involving a relationship between organisms and the environment
[5] **trend:** a pattern; a general direction or tendency

CUES TO RECOGNIZE CONCLUSIONS

1. Words that signal a forthcoming summary, logical conclusion, or ending:

   Consequently, . . .
   In conclusion, . . .
   In the final analysis, . . .
   Okay, . . . that completes X
   So, . . .
   So remember. . .
   The bottom line is . . .
   Therefore, . . .
   Thus, . . .
   To sum up (in a few words), . . .

2. Words or phrases that tie together previously stated ideas:

   For (all of) these reasons, . . .
   These examples (serve to) show . . .
   What all this proves is . . .

Exercise 2

You will hear the conclusions of five different lectures. First, read the question about each excerpt. Then listen to the excerpt. After listening, answer the questions or check (✓) the best answer or answers.

Example

This was a lecture on stress. What topics did the lecturer cover in the lecture?

_____ **a.** Problems are in the ways that we cope with stress, not the stress itself

_____ **b.** Stress can be positive or negative

_____ **c.** There are several strategies for dealing with stress

_____ **d.** All of the above

The lecturer said:

Okay . . so remember . . . the problem is not in the stressful experiences themselves . . . we all experience stress and stressful events . . . the problem is in one's reaction to these experiences . . . and each of us has our own limits for stress . . . our own ways of coping with stress . . . our own way of balancing the cost and benefits of stress . . . stress can be positive for some . . . more positive for others . . . negative for some . . . etc. . . . perhaps your strategies for dealing with stress were mentioned in this lecture . . . and perhaps some of you have your own ways that you'd like to share with the class . . . so, uh, why don't we open the floor to comments . . . suggestions . . . questions from you before we go on.

The correct answer is (d).

1. This was in a math lecture. What has the lecturer finished talking about?

   _____

   What is the lecturer ready to begin? _____

2. This was in a lecture about psychology. What has the lecturer finished talking about for the moment?

   _____

   What new topic is he introducing? _____

cactus (pl.: *cacti*)

3. This was in a lecture on ecology. What has the lecturer finished talking about? Check (✓) one or more answers.

   ____ a. One particular kind of cactus found in southern California

   ____ b. Different cacti found in southern California

   ____ c. Different cacti found around the world

   ____ d. The lack of life in deserts

4. This was from a lecture about brain research. What point(s) did the professor make in the conclusion? Check (✓) one or more answers.

   ____ a. Mental activity is important for maintaining brain power.

   ____ b. Physical activity is important for maintaining brain power.

   ____ c. Physical activity is equally important for young and old people (as it relates to brain power).

   ____ d. If you don't use your brain power, you'll lose it!

5. This was in a political science lecture on Amnesty International, a human rights organization. What has the lecturer finished talking about? Check (✓) one or more answers.

   ____ a. Eight people who have helped Amnesty International grow strong

   ____ b. Eight principles underlying Amnesty International's work

   ____ c. Eight different countries in which Amnesty International has recently worked

   ____ d. Eight reasons people should support Amnesty International

Did you know?

Amnesty International began in 1961 and now has 2.2 million members.

C Recognizing Digressions

When people write, they have time to edit their words and eliminate information that does not fit. When people speak, this is impossible. Speakers more frequently and more easily digress; that is, they wander or move away from the main point. This may be an intentional digression, such as an interesting story, a joke, or an important piece of information that suddenly comes to mind. It may also be unintentional, such as when speakers go from one point to another and eventually find themselves far from the intended topic.

As a listener, you need to recognize digressions so that they do not confuse you and distract you from the key points of the lecture. Digressions can also provide a lighthearted break from continuous note-taking.

Although digressions are sometimes preceded by specific cues ("This reminds me of a funny story"), more often they are not. However, cues are often used *after* a digression to bring the audience back to the original subject.

LISTENING AND NOTE-TAKING STRATEGY

Digressions give you an opportunity to relax your active note-taking. Listen for the cues that tell you that the lecturer is coming back to the topic and when you need to start listening and taking notes actively again.

CUES TO RECOGNIZE DIGRESSIONS

1. Phrases or sentences that signal a possible digression:

   Now before I go on, . . .
   By the way, . . .
   Let me talk about X for a minute.
   Speaking of X . . .
   That reminds me of a story.

2. Words or phrases that follow a digression:

   Now, . . .
   Anyway, . . .
   Okay, . . .
   Back to (what we were talking about) . . .

3. Rhetorical questions that follow a digression and signal a return to the original subject:

   What were we talking about?
   Where were we?

Exercise 3

You will hear five lecture excerpts that include a digression. First, read the questions about each excerpt. Then listen to the excerpt without taking notes. After listening, answer the questions.

1. This was from a lecture on the theory of the aquatic[1] evolution[2] of humans. In the main part of the lecture, the speaker talks about his view that humans have descended from aquatic animals as well as land-based animals.

   What is the digression?

   _____

   Would this information be important to note? _____

2. This was from an ecology lecture on the moderating[3] effect of water on the climate. In the main part of the lecture, the speaker talks about the two factors related to why water has a moderating effect on climate: (a) its specific heat and (b) the two forms of latent heat.

   What is the digression?

   _____

   Would this information be important to note? _____

3. This was from an ecology lecture on desert life. In the main part of the lecture, the speaker introduces her topic: cacti.

   What is the digression?

   _____

   Would this information be important to note? _____

4. This was from an economics lecture. In the main part of the lecture, the professor defines the terms *bull market* and *bear market*.

   What is the digression?

   _____

   Would this information be important to note? _____

5. This was from a lecture on psychology. In the main part of the lecture, the speaker introduces the topic: Kohlberg's theory of moral development. He says he is going to ask two questions to help students apply this topic in real life: Why are you in college? Why are you taking a Friday morning class?

   What is the digression?

   _____

   Would this information be important to note? _____

---

[1] *aquatic:* relating to water
[2] *evolution:* a gradual development
[3] *moderate something:* to make something less strong or extreme

THE BASICS OF NOTE-TAKING

Goals

- Learn to choose key words to note
- Learn to use abbreviations and symbols in notes
- Learn to visually represent the relative importance of information
- Learn to visually represent the relationship between pieces of information

DISCUSSION

Note-Taking

1. Do you think you are a good note-taker in your native language? Why or why not?

2. When you take notes in your native language, do you try to write down every word? If not, how do you decide what to write down? Do you use the same method in English? Why or why not?

3. Do you review your notes after a lecture? When and how often?

4. Do you ever compare your notes with other students? Why or why not?

5. Do you ever record your lectures? Why or why not?

When you take notes, you do not have time to write down everything that the speaker says. You must note as much information as possible in the fewest words. These few important words that carry the main meaning are **key words**.

Notice how key words are noted in the following example.

> LECTURER: *The Sahara desert is the largest desert in the world . . . it's huge . . . enormous . . . and it's getting larger every day!*
>
> NOTES: *Sahara—largest desert in world—getting larger!*

Notice how the verb *be* is not important and does not need to be noted. Synonyms or repeated words don't need to be noted either.

What words *are* important to note? Typically, nouns, active verbs, and adjectives are key words. Also, typically, articles and digressions are *not* important to note. As mentioned in Unit 2, paraphrases and repetitions indicate important ideas, but you do not need to note those same key words multiple times.

Choosing key words to note also greatly depends on the context. For example, prepositions are usually not key words, although they can be.

In the example below, the preposition "on" is not important.

> LECTURER: *JFK was assassinated on November 22, 1963.*
>
> NOTES: *JFK assassinated 11/22/63.*

However, in the following case, the preposition "on" *is* a key word.

> LECTURER: *Often storks build their nests on chimney tops . . . and these nests are big.*
>
> NOTES: *Stork nests on chimney tops—BIG!*

USUALLY KEY WORDS	USUALLY NOT KEY WORDS
• **nouns**, especially names and dates (*Napoleon Bonaparte, 1066 , earthquakes*) • **active verbs** (*created, fought, discovered*) • **adjectives** and **adverbs**, especially comparatives and superlatives (*large, least common*)	• pronouns (*he, she*) • the verb **be** (*was, is*) • prepositions (*to, in, at, of*) • articles (*a, an, the*) • repeated words or paraphrases (*large: really big, huge, enormous*) • digressions (*that reminds me of the time when my daughter gave me a rose . . .*)

NOTE-TAKING STRATEGY

Do not try to note every word. Note key words. Try to get as much information as possible in the fewest words. Do not spend time correcting your grammar or spelling.

B Using Abbreviations Thoughtfully

It is important that you can understand your notes a day, a week, or even a year later. Be careful with abbreviations.

LECTURER: *John F. Kennedy was the thirty-fifth president of the United States.*

NOTES: JFK — 35th pres. of U.S.

JFK are initials that are familiar to most Americans, so it makes sense to use them. Compare the following two sets of notes.

LECTURER: *Dick Cheney was George W. Bush's vice-president.*

GOOD NOTES: Cheney — G.W. Bush's V.P.

POOR NOTES: DC — GWB's V.P.

NOTE-TAKING STRATEGY

Use abbreviations if you know that you will be able to recognize them later.

What is wrong with the second example? The initials "DC" and "GWB" are not familiar, and you might not know what they mean if you read your notes later. You are, however, probably familiar with "V.P.", the abbreviation for "vice-president."

Using Note-Taking Symbols and Abbreviations

Symbols can replace words that show relationships. For example, the dash (—) can symbolize *was* or any other form of the verb *be*.

Example

JFK — 35th pres. of U.S. = John F. Kennedy *was* the thirty-fifth president of the United States.

Here are some other symbols that you might use:

=	equals	/	per
≠	does not equal	~	approximately; about
&	and	→1929	since 1929
>	is more than	←1929	1929 and earlier
<	is less than	c.	century
$	money	w/	with
↑	go up; increase	w/o	without
↓	go down; decrease	♂	man; men
→	leading to; heading toward	♀	woman; women
∴	therefore; so	e.g.	for example
Y?	why	" "	(repeated words)
∵ OR b/c	because	#	number
"	inches	i.e.	that is; in other words
'	feet	%	percent
o	degree	+	plus; and
@	at	* OR !	Important!

Do you use any other symbols? Share them with the class. Note any additional symbols that you would like to remember in the space below.

Exercise

You will hear ten short statements. Take notes in as few words as possible. Use note-taking symbols and abbreviations where appropriate. When you are finished, compare and explain your notes in small groups.

Example

LECTURER: *The demand for oil has increased greatly in the past 100 years so the price has also risen.*

NOTES: demand for oil ↑ past 100 yrs.   ∴ price ↑

1.	6.
2.	7.
3.	8.
4.	9.
5.	10.

D Visually Representing Relationships and the Relative Importance of Information

Another way to increase the amount of information in your notes is to use the space on your paper to show relationships and the relative importance of information.

Example

LECTURER: *The three largest states in the United States are Texas, Alaska, and California. Texas is located in the south-central part of the United States and is on the border of Mexico. Alaska is located to the northwest of Canada, and California is on the western coast of the continental United States.*

NOTES:

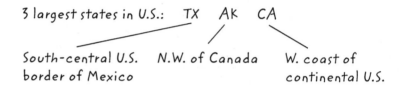

OR:

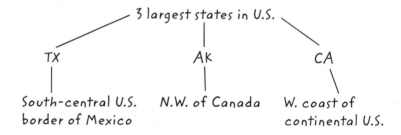

Notice how the arrangement of the notes clearly shows which ideas are related to one another.

Indentation is another way to show the relationships between pieces of information and their relative importance. Write the most general information farthest to the left. Write more specific information under the general information and indent it toward the right.

Example

LECTURER: *A poll was taken in 2007 asking people in a number of different countries questions about whether they rate men and women equally as good political leaders . . . here's what they found out . . . they found that in the U.S. . . . . fully three-quarters say that they make equally good leaders . . . in Sweden . . . Swedes in the greatest numbers felt that men and women were equal. . . . Nine out of ten believe this to be true. . . . Now Sweden also has the highest scores on female political empowerment . . . that's a measure of how much women play leadership roles in a place . . . so there's probably a correlation there . . .*

poll (2007): ♀ ♂ = as leaders?

U.S.: $\frac{3}{4}$ say =

Sweden: 9/10 "   "

Has ↑ score   "♀ polit. empowerment"

(measure of ♀ in leader roles)

Correlation?

There are other ways to arrange this information into notes. In all cases, make sure that you use as few words as possible and accurately express the lecturer's ideas in terms of importance of information and relationship between pieces of information.

NOTE-TAKING STRATEGY

Use the space on the page to make important information immediately clear and to show how ideas relate to one another.

Exercise 2

You will hear ten short statements. On a separate piece of paper, take informative notes in as few words as possible. Use symbols, abbreviations, key words, indentation, and connecting lines where appropriate. When you are finished, compare and explain your notes in small groups.

"Nu Shu": Women's Unique Language (Linguistics)

ACTIVITY **1** **LISTENING AND READING**

🎧 In Unit 2, you practiced predicting content and lecture direction while reading a transcript of a lecture on *nu shu*. You will now listen to the entire lecture. While listening, look at the example notes below.

Nu Shu—Chinese for "♀'s writing"

   — used only by ♀

   — only one in existence?

   — <10 people fluently read/write it... # ↓

   — existed centuries (attn.—last few decades)

Origins?—???

   — 3ʳᵈ c. remote south central China?

   — 1,000 yrs. ago . . . Emperor's concubine?

Why created?

   — in past ♂ read/write Chinese

   — ♀'s freedom ltd. physically + socially

        bound feet   after marriage → husband's family/distance

   — ∴ ♀ needed way to communicate w/ ♀

     — script passed ♀ to ♀ (generations/friends)

     — hid words in notes, fans, "3ʳᵈ Day Book"

        — diaries given to ♀ when marry, expressed mother's/
          friends' wishes, + blank pages to write experience

     — many buried w/♀

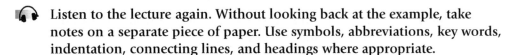

Did you know?

In the 4th grade in China, children are expected to know 2000 written characters!

Characteristics?

　— Like Chinese — write top → bottom, read right → left

　— unlike " " — characters represent SOUND, not idea

　　　　　— characters more delicate, elongated

　　　　　— fewer characters
　　　　　(1800–2500 vs. 30,000 in Mandarin)

Situation now?

　— all read/write Chinese now so ♀ don't need nu shu

　— scholars interested in learning lang. / thoughts of ♀ fr. past

　　— compiling dictionary

　— COMMERCIAL interest!

　　— foundation donate $ for museum to preserve nu shu

　　— HK co. invest $ for roads, hotels in nu shu part of China
　　　　　↓

　— changing relations there betw. ♀ & ♂

　　Why?　　　♀ bringing in $ w/ researchers/ tourists

　　　　　　　♀ → center of ec. & cult. life!

　　　　　　　♀ power ↑ !!!

Did you notice the following?

- The lecturer began with some introductory comments asking students if they had heard of *nu shu*, but the note-taker waited to take notes until specific facts were presented.

- The notes visually represent the organization of the lecture and the relative importance of pieces of information in the lecture. The major points are written farthest to the left, with details indented under the generalizations that they support.

- Headings such as "Origins," "Why Created?," "Characteristics," and "Situation Now" help to organize the notes by clarifying the purpose of important sections.

ACTIVITY 2 **LISTENING AND NOTE-TAKING**

Listen to the lecture again. Without looking back at the example, take notes on a separate piece of paper. Use symbols, abbreviations, key words, indentation, connecting lines, and headings where appropriate.

E

Eight DOs and DON'Ts for Improving Lecture Comprehension and Note-Taking

1. **DON'T** note every word.	**DO** note key words. Remember that nouns, active verbs, and adjectives are usually most important.
2. **DON'T** write complete words.	**DO** use abbreviations and symbols.
3. **DON'T** note indiscriminately.	**DO** evaluate as you listen. Decide what is important and what is not.
4. **DON'T** take notes as if you were writing a composition.	**DO** use the space on your paper to organize information and visually represent the relationship between ideas.
5. **DON'T** be a passive listener.	**DO** be an active listener. Predict lecture content and organization.
6. **DON'T** give up if you miss information.	**DO** make guesses if you miss information. Remember that lecturers usually repeat and paraphrase information.
7. **DON'T** lose sight of the forest for the trees. (Don't listen for details before getting the larger picture.)	**DO** listen for the lecturer's main points and for the general organizational framework.
8. **DON'T** forget about your notes when you leave the lecture.	**DO** rewrite and/or revise your notes as soon as possible after the lecture. That way, ideas that you did not have time to note will still be fresh in your mind and you will be able to add them. In addition, you can reorganize information so that the ideas are more clearly and accurately represented.

How does this cartoon demonstrate the meaning of the idiom "to lose sight of the forest for the trees"?

NOTING NUMBERS AND STATISTICS

Stop by my apartment. I'm at 2351 E. 203rd St., Apt 334, but if I'm not home call me on my cell at 888-555-0037 extension 21240. Okay?

Goals

- Learn how to recognize the differences between numbers that sound similar
- Learn how to comprehend and note large numbers, fractions, decimals, ratios, and dates
- Practice noting numbers, dates, and statistics while listening to lectures

DISCUSSION

Numbers

1. What is your major or expected major at the university? What kinds of numbers are commonly used in lectures in that field (e.g., ages, measurements, dates, statistics, fractions, decimals, percentages, ratios, equations)?

2. Of these different kinds of numbers, which are the easiest for you to comprehend and note? Which are the most difficult? If numbers are difficult for you, what makes them difficult?

3. Have you ever conducted a survey? If so, what was it about, and what were your findings? How important are surveys, questionnaires, or research data in your major?

4. In what subjects or fields can you expect to find lots of dates? measurements? equations? surveys and questionnaires? other research data?

A   Differentiating between Numbers That Sound Similar

Hearing the difference between numbers such as *fourteen* and *forty* requires paying attention to differences in stress. Listen to the following numbers.

14 *fourteen*	40 *forty*	17 *seventeen*	70 *seventy*
15 *fifteen*	50 *fifty*	18 *eighteen*	80 *eighty*
16 *sixteen*	60 *sixty*	19 *nineteen*	90 *ninety*

Exercise 1

You will hear ten numbers. First say all of the numbers out loud. Then listen and circle the numbers that you hear.

1.	13	30	33	6.	18	80	8
2.	14	40	4	7.	19	90	9
3.	15	50	5	8.	14	40	44
4.	16	60	6	9.	16	60	66
5.	17	70	7	10.	18	80	8

Exercise 2

You will hear six numbers. Write the numbers that you hear.

1. _____ 4. _____

2. _____ 5. _____

3. _____ 6. _____

B   Noting Years

Notice the following ways to present years.

1300 B.C. *or* B.C.E	thirteen hundred B.C. *or* B.C.E.
1492 A.D. *or* C.E.	fourteen (hundred and) ninety-two A.D. *or* C.E.
1902	nineteen oh two
2000	two thousand
2014	two thousand (and) fourteen; twenty-fourteen
the 14th c.	the fourteenth century (1300–1399)
the '60s	(the decade of) the sixties, the nineteen sixties (1960–1969)

Exercise

🎧 **You will hear ten years. Write the years that you hear.**

1. 1605
2. 1827
3. 2014
4. 1920
5. 1850

6. 1502
7. 1589
8. 1870
9. 1808
10. 2001

C Noting Large Numbers in Isolation

Noting large numbers requires familiarity with the English number system. The basics of the system are as follows:

100	one hundred *or* a hundred
1,000	one thousand *or* a thousand
10,000	ten thousand
100,000	one hundred thousand *or* a hundred thousand
1,000,000	one million *or* a million
10,000,000	ten million
100,000,000	one hundred million *or* a hundred million
1,000,000,000	one billion *or* a billion

Look at the number 12,506,825,001.

12,	506,	825,	001
(Billions)	(Millions)	(Thousands)	(Ones)

You can read this as "12 billion, 506 million, 825 thousand, (and) one."

Now look at this number: 1,215,750,030.

1,	215,	750,	030
(Billions)	(Millions)	(Thousands)	(Ones)

You can read this as "1 billion, 215 million, 750 thousand, (and) 30."

Here is one more: 250,327,919,321.

250,	327,	919,	321
(Billions)	(Millions)	(Thousands)	(Ones)

You can read this as "250 billion, 327 million, 919 thousand, 3 hundred, (and) 21."

Remember that numbers are in groups of three digits, except for numbers under 100 and the group farthest to the left. It may help you to write a comma (,) every time you hear a word such as "billion," "million," or "thousand." You will usually hear a pause after these words.

The "group of three" concept is very important for numbers such as 100,001. The zeros are necessary to hold the places in the group. In this case, the number 100 is in the thousands group and the number 1 is in the ones group. The ones group has three places; therefore the number 1 must be written as 001.

Note that some large numbers can be stated in fractions:

4,250,000 = four and a quarter million *or* four million two hundred fifty thousand
10,500,000 = ten and a half million *or* ten million five hundred thousand

Exercise 4

You will hear ten numbers. First say all of the numbers out loud. Then listen and circle the numbers that you hear.

1. (102)	120	1,002
2. 115	(150)	1,050
3. (1,020)	1,200	1,002
4. 1,252	(1,250)	1,025
5. 3,560	3,516	(3,056)
6. (53,000)	50,300	503,000
7. 45,000,000	4,000,500	(4,500,000)
8. (1,213,000)	1,000,213,000	(1,213,000,000)
9. 5,000,000	(50,000,000)	5,000,000,000
10. 8,500,000	85,000,000	(85,000,000,000)

Exercise 5

You will hear ten numbers. Write the numbers that you hear.

1. 14,569
2. 67,440
3. 15,515
4. 2.000.001
5. 2,000.100

6. 202.202.000
7. a? 95.825.00 0
8. 95.925,000,000
9. t̶o̶ 175,240,150
10. 12.000.565.000

D Noting Fractions and Decimals

Notice the following ways to say fractions and decimals.

$\frac{1}{2}$ one-half

$\frac{2}{3}$ two-thirds

$\frac{3}{4}$ three-quarters *or* three-fourths

$\frac{5}{8}$ five-eighths

$5\frac{1}{8}$ five and an eighth *or* five and one-eighth

5.8   five point eight

3.14   three point one four

.002   point oh oh two

Exercise 6

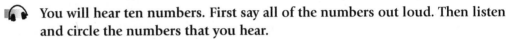

You will hear ten numbers. First say all of the numbers out loud. Then listen and circle the numbers that you hear.

1. $\boxed{\frac{4}{5}}$ 45 $4\frac{1}{5}$ 4.5   6. $\frac{3}{4}$ 304 $3\frac{3}{4}$ (3.4)

2. $\frac{2}{8}$ 208 $\left(2\frac{1}{8}\right)$ 2.8   7. $\frac{7}{8}$ (78) $7\frac{1}{8}$ 7.8

3. $\frac{2}{5}$ 25 $2\frac{1}{5}$ (2.5)   8. $\left(\frac{2}{3}\right)$ 23 $2\frac{1}{3}$ 2.3

4. $\frac{1}{3}$ 30 $\left(1\frac{1}{3}\right)$ 1.3   9. $\frac{3}{5}$ (35) $3\frac{1}{5}$ 3.5

5. $\frac{1}{6}$ (106) $1\frac{1}{6}$ 1.6   10. $\frac{2}{6}$ 206 $2\frac{1}{6}$ (2.6)

Exercise 7

You will hear ten numbers. Write the numbers that you hear.

1. _____ $\frac{1}{8}$ _____   6. _____ $3\frac{3}{4}$ _____

2. _____ 1.8 _____   7. _____ 8.27 _____

3. _____ $3\frac{1}{8}$ _____   8. _____ $2\frac{2}{3}$ _____

4. _____ 308 _____   9. _____ 78 _____

5. _____ 3/4 _____   10. _____ 2.056 _____

E Noting Ratios

Notice the following ways to talk about ratios or proportions.

2 per 10   =   two in ten   =   two out of ten

O O X X X X X X X X

5:1   =   five to one

O O O O O X

Exercise 8

You will hear five ratios or proportions. Write the numbers that you hear.

1. In 2007, nearly ___3 in 10___ Americans listed reading as one of their favorite leisure activities.

2. In the same study, ___18 out of 100 / 18%___ Americans listed TV watching.

3. And in the same study, people preferred computer activities to bicycling ___3 : 1___ .

4. In 2008, worldwide, nearly ___2 per 3 / 2/3___ city dwellers lived in cities with populations of 1 million or fewer.

5. The number of infant deaths in Ethiopia in 2007 was ___77 per 1000___ births.

Exploring a Market: Attitudes toward Pets
(Business/Sociology)

Vocabulary
Related to Business and Marketing

Check (✓) the words you know. Underline the words you want to learn. Then check their meaning with your instructor or in a dictionary.

market X (to a group)

investment
business ventures

income
revenue
profit

expenditures

market forecast
market outlook
market predictions

market research
focus groups
demographic groups

market outreach
advertising campaigns

generations
Baby Boomers
Gen-X

sector, subsector

ACTIVITY **1** **PRE-LECTURE DISCUSSION**

Discuss the following questions in small groups.

1. In the United States, the majority of pet owners consider their pets "members of the family." What does this mean? Is this your attitude? Is this attitude shared by members of other cultures you are familiar with?

2. What pets do you have? What pets have you had?

3. In what ways might pets be "big business" in the United States and elsewhere?

4. Why do people like animals? Below are a few quotes about animals. What reasons are given for liking animals in general or specific animals? Can you think of others?

I like pigs. Dogs look up to us. Cats look down on us. Pigs treat us as equals.

  —Winston Churchill, English prime minister (1874–1965)

A cat has absolute emotional honesty: human beings, for one reason or another, may hide their feelings, but a cat does not.

  —Ernest Hemingway, American author (1899–1961)

If animals could speak the dog would be a blundering outspoken fellow, but the cat would have the rare grace of never saying a word too much.

  —Mark Twain, American author (1835–1910)

Animals are such agreeable friends—they ask no questions, they pass no criticisms.

—George Eliot, English author (1819–1880)

An animal's eyes have the power to speak a great language.

—Martin Buber, Austrian philosopher (1878–1965)

It is much easier to show compassion to animals. They are never wicked.

—Haile Selassie, Ethiopian emperor (1891–1975)

Until one has loved an animal, a part of one's soul remains unawakened.

—Anatole France, French author (1844–1924)

What is man without the beasts? If all the beasts were gone, men would die from loneliness of spirit. For whatever happens to the beasts happens to man. All things are connected.

—Chief Seattle, Native American chief (1786–1866)

ACTIVITY **2** **PREPARING FOR THE LECTURE**

The title of the lecture is "Exploring a Market: Attitudes toward Pets." What do you expect the lecturer to tell you in the lecture? Brainstorm ideas with your classmates.

Listen to the introduction. Then answer the question. Check (✓) the correct answer.

What will the lecturer *not* talk about?

__Yes__ **a.** Some data from a survey about pets in people's lives

__No__ **b.** How data from a survey relates to marketing and investment

__Yes__ **c.** The idea of pets as a cultural phenomena

__No__ **d.** Studies about the benefits of pets in our lives

---

ACTIVITY **3** **LISTENING AND NOTE-TAKING**

Polls, surveys, questionnaires, and focus groups are used in many disciplines. In the area of business, data from these sources help drive business decisions regarding where to invest and where and how to advertise. Often, analysis of data leads to marketing campaigns targeting particular sectors of the population (e.g., women versus men, children versus adults, and so on).

The lecture you will hear describes a poll about Americans and their pets. Information about changes in attitudes and spending habits that have occurred in China is given toward the end of the lecture.

Listen to the lecture and take notes in the box on the following page. Focus on the main ideas: the survey, its purpose, and its results.

Vocabulary
Related to Polls or Surveys

Check (✓) the words you know. Underline the words you want to learn. Then check their meaning with your instructor or in a dictionary.

poll
survey

rank items
(take a) poll/survey

respondent

random sample

margin of error

Survey data

Draw conclusions, make predictions about markets; investment decisions

- # owned dogs U.S.: _74, 8 M_
- # " cats ": _19 M_
- spending on pets = _36 M_ in 200_6_
  - on _food, healthcar, laundries,_
- industry = one of fastest growing subsectors in U.S. econ: _6% yer_

Survey about _____ (200_7_): _____ adults

Looked at _8 education._

Age groups: Baby Boomers: born _2000 - 2002_

Gen X: " _1965 - 1966_

Echo Boomers: " _1967 - 1989_

Matures: " _before 1945_

Who has a pet? _65%_ Americans

What kinds of pets?
- dogs & cats most popular
- fish: _15%_ — bird: _7%_ — other type pet: _12%_
- _13%_ own 6+ pets!

Pet member of family?
88% / 7% / 47% not sure

What do w/ pet?
69% like dogs sleep with then, 78% sleep with cats.

Disclaimer:
2/3 holiday.

China? (fr. market research newsletter)
5 M increase pets in 2003 - 2004.

Implications for market outreach? Investment? Advertise?

ACTIVITY **4** **REPLAY QUESTIONS**

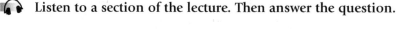 **Listen to a section of the lecture. Then answer the question.**

1. What is the professor's attitude about people who choose to have lots of animals? Check (✓) one.

   ✓ a. She understands their behavior because she has a cousin who does the same.

   ____ b. It is difficult for her to understand their behavior.

   ____ c. She admires them because she likes to imagine having a lot of pets.

   ____ d. She dislikes them because she does not believe in pet ownership.

2. What does the lecturer mean by "take this survey with a grain of salt"?

   _____

Did you know?

The lifespan of the common goldfish is 20 years. It has an attention span of 3 seconds!

ACTIVITY **5** **"OTHER VOICES" FOLLOW-UP**

The professor asked if there were any questions. One student responded. Listen to the conversation and answer the questions.

1. What did the student want to know? Check (✓) one.

   ____ a. Why the Chinese have not had a tradition of pets

   ✓ b. Why attitudes and habits relating to pets have been changing in China

   ____ c. What additional changes relating to pet ownership and spending are expected in China in the near future

   ____ d. Whether pet ownership is limited to specific areas in China, such as large cities

2. Which ideas were mentioned in the class discussion answering this question? Check (✓) one or more.

   ____ a. The Chinese never had pets before because they felt they were unclean.

   ✓ b. More Chinese see pets as an extension of the family, not just animals.

   ✓ c. More Chinese see pets as companions.

   ✓ d. Changes in Chinese attitudes toward pets have occurred because of smaller family size.

_____ e. In China, people who live in the countryside tend to have more pets than urban dwellers (i.e., people who live in cities).

✓ f. More Chinese young people see pet ownership as a fashion and identity statement.

✓ g. More Chinese are looking to pets to relieve stress and loneliness.

_____ h. Apartments in cities have become larger so there is more room for animals.

_____ i. The Chinese will start wanting multiple animals in the near future.

3. In many university classes, professors welcome thoughtful questions from students. Imagine you are a student in this class. Write one follow-up question that you might ask related to the lecture topic.

~~å~~ why always people live mor having a dog instead another pet?

ACTIVITY 6 **USING YOUR NOTES**

Use your notes to determine whether each statement is true (_T_) or false (_F_). If you think the statement is false, be prepared to correct the statement.

_____ 1. There are almost 75,000,000,000 owned dogs in the United States.

_____ 2. There are approximately 19 million owned cats in the United States.

_____ 3. The pet industry is growing in the United States by as much as 16 percent a year.

_____ 4. Nearly two out of three Americans currently have a pet.

_____ 5. The likelihood of having a pet decreases as education level increases.

_____ 6. African Americans tend to have pets more often than other racial/ethnic groups.

_____ 7. The poll divided the survey group into four demographic groups according to age.

_____ 8. There are more dog owners than cat owners.

_____ 9. Seventy percent of pet owners have a dog.

_____ 10. Women are more likely than men to consider their pets members of their family.

_____ 11. Most Americans who have pets consider them members of the family.

_____ 12. More people let their cats sleep on their bed than let their dogs sleep on their bed.

_____ 13. The increasing popularity of pets is purely a Western phenomenon.

_____ 14. China's pet population grew by more than 50 million animals in a five-year time span.

_____ 15. More people own cats than dogs in China.

_____ 16. The sale of dog and cat food in China grew by 30 percent from 2003 to 2004.

_____ 17. The survey was done in person at a mall.

_____ 18. The number of adults surveyed was 2,455.

Compare with your classmates your answers to the preceding questions. If you have different answers, check your notes and discuss your reasons for making your choices.

ACTIVITY **8** **POST-LECTURE DISCUSSION**

Discuss the following questions in small groups.

1. Do the findings of these polls sound right to you? Were you surprised about anything?

2. How do the findings compare to your own experience?

3. Given the information that you heard, what kinds of industries would you consider investing in? What kind of advertising would you do and who would you target in your marketing campaign?

ACTIVITY **9** **ACADEMIC WORD LIST VOCABULARY**[1]

Match the word and its meaning. Write the correct letter in the space provided. (An example is given to help you see the word in context.)

Group 1
  a. viewpoint
  b. any of the different age levels in a family (e.g., grandparents, children)
  c. consequences; results
  d. related to group characteristics, such as race, country of origin, religion, or culture
  e. facts, events, or images that attract interest

_e_ 1. *phenomena*[2]   How do you explain phenomena such as low voter turnout?

_b_ 2. *generation*   Fashions vary from generation to generation.

_a_ 3. *perspective*   He has an unusual perspective on that situation.

_d_ 4. *ethnicity*   What is his ethnicity? Is he Asian or Caucasian?

_c_ 5. *implications*   There are serious implications if that information is true.

---

[1] The Academic Word List was developed in 2000 by Averil Coxhead from written material used in the fields of liberal arts, commerce, law, and science. Familiarity with the most common words from this list will help you better understand the language that you encounter in classes and textbooks. The words in this exercise come from the lecture you just heard. Throughout this book, additional words from the Academic Word List are marked with an asterisk (*).

[2] *Phenomena* is plural; the singular is *phenomenon*

Group 2

a. to concentrate; to pay attention
b. to put money into (in the hopes of future profit or earnings)
c. to develop (toward mental or physical potential)
d. to poll; to examine the opinions of a group of people by asking them something and recording answers
e. to differ

__d__ 6. *survey* Let's survey our clients to see what they want.

__b__ 7. *invest* In this economic climate, where should we invest?

__c__ 8. *mature* As children mature, they develop a clearer sense of their own needs.

__e__ 9. *vary* Answers vary from person to person depending on their situation.

__a__ 10. *focus* We need to focus more on this problem.

Group 3

a. relating to data and other numbers
b. focused on a particular, not generalizations
c. happening by chance, without following rules
d. not exactly; not precisely
e. relating to a specific geographic area

__c__ 11. *randomly* They chose the participants randomly.

__d__ 12. *approximately* Approximately 5 million people live in that city.

__b__ 13. *specifically* I asked her to specifically comment on the buying habits of teenagers.

__e__ 14. *regionally* Regionally, we see differences in preferences.

__a__ 15. *statistically* The chances of winning a lottery are statistically low.

VOCABULARY LEARNING STRATEGY

Active vocabulary learners are always "on the lookout" for new words to learn. They consciously rehearse and practice words.

Read the following conversation between two venture capitalists (people or businesses who invest in start-up or new businesses). Fill in the blanks with vocabulary below. Use each word only once.

| sectors* | investment* | campaign | research* |

A: I'm considering a(n) ___investment___ in a start-up company
   (1.)
   that has designed and wants to market a line of clothing for pets. Are you
   interested?

B: I'd have to think about it. What kind of ___research___ has been
   (2.)
   done to show that there is a need for this type of business?

A: First of all, statistics show that the pet industry is one of the fastest-growing
   ___sectors___ in the entire U.S. economy. On top of that, I've
   (3.)
   recently seen the results of a survey that showed that more than two-thirds
   of pet owners have bought their pets holiday presents.

B: But clothes?

A: Not yet. But I think that if we put together the right kind of TV and media
   advertising ___campaign___ and target the right demographic
   (4.)
   groups, particularly the younger generation, it could work.

B: Hmmm. Let me sleep on it.

Listen to the conversation to check your answers.

ACTIVITY 11 **RETAINING VOCABULARY**

Write at least five words from this lecture unit that you would like to remember. Use each word in an example that will remind you of its meaning.

Example

poll: the polls showed that the majority of the people supported the
president

1. _____

   _____

2. _____

   _____

3. _____

_____

4. _____

_____

5. _____

_____

ACTIVITY 12 **BEYOND THE LECTURE: SPEAKING, LISTENING, SURFING THE NET**

Complete one of these assignments.

1. Create a questionnaire to survey your classmates about their habits. You may focus, for example, on habits related to studying, eating, or recreation. Distribute the questionnaire to your classmates. Once you have collected and compiled the results, present them to your classmates in percentage form and have them take notes.

2. Harris Polls and Gallup Polls are two U.S.-based market research groups that can be found online at http://www.harrispollonline.com and http://www.gallup.com, respectively. Explore their Web sites—or similar ones—to find a poll about something that interests you. Prepare to talk with your classmates for two to three minutes about the poll and its results. Use the chart below to help organize your presentation.

General Topic of Poll:

Date and Location of Poll:

Respondent Characteristics:

Findings of Poll:

Tobacco through the Millennia (Agriculture/History)

Vocabulary

Related to Agriculture

Check (✓) the words you know. Underline the words you want to learn. Then check their meaning with your instructor or in a dictionary.

crop

farms
orchards
plantations

cultivate
irrigate
plow
harvest
sow

soil
fertilizer
amendment

insecticide
pesticide

agribusiness
import
export
process
manufacture

T A B A C O L O G I A.   7

Mascula sum Peti species; praestantior herba
Me nusquam in terris; hinc Panacea vocor.

Huron Indian myth has it that in ancient times, when the land was barren and the people were starving, the Great Spirit sent forth a woman to save humanity. As she traveled over the world, everywhere her right hand touched the soil, there grew potatoes. And everywhere her left hand touched the soil, there grew corn. And when the world was rich and fertile, she sat down and rested. When she arose, there grew tobacco. . . . [1]

---

[1] Gene Borio, Tobacco Timeline: http://www.tobacco.org/resources/history/Tobacco_History.html.

ACTIVITY 1 PRE-LECTURE DISCUSSION

Discuss the following questions in small groups.

1. What food items have been particularly important in your culture's diet?

2. The Huron Indians (an indigenous group in North America) tell a myth (see previous page) about the origins of potatoes, corn, and tobacco. The following are a couple more examples of stories telling about a food's origins.

> **Popcorn:** Old-timers tell a story about a summer that was so hot that the corn in the fields started to pop right off the stalks. What a tasty surprise!
>
> **Potato chips:** In 1853, Native American George Crum was a chef in New York. When a customer complained that his French fries were too thick, Mr. Crum sliced them paper thin and fried them until they were crunchy: the first potato chips![2]

Do you know of any other myths, legends, or stories that describe the creation of any particular food, drink, or crop?

ACTIVITY 2 PREPARING FOR THE LECTURE

Listen to the introduction to the lecture. Then answer the questions.

1. The lecturer says, "If I asked you to free-associate with the word *tobacco*, what would come up?" What are the first three things that come to your mind if someone says the word *tobacco*?

   The lecturer also says that "Your answer would have a lot to do with who you are . . . where you live, where you were brought up, what century you were brought up in." What does the lecturer mean? Did the three things that you named reflect those things?

2. What is your personal experience with and attitude about tobacco use?

3. What will the lecture focus on? Check (✓) one.

   ____ **a.** The dangers of tobacco use

   ____ **b.** The history of cigarettes

   ✓ **c.** The history of tobacco

   ____ **d.** The marketing of tobacco

4. The title of this lecture is "Tobacco through the Millennia." What do you know about the real history of tobacco, from the distant past (thousands of years ago) to the modern day?

---

[2] History of Food and Food Products: http://inventors.about.com/od/foodrelatedinventions/History_of_Food_and_Food_Products.htm.

The lecture you will hear tells about tobacco and its impact over the millennia. The lecture contains many dates. Focus on the dates and what happened then. Add details as you can. Take notes in the box below. (Before listening and noting, review the notes to make sure you understand the vocabulary.)

Tobacco
History:

Product? Crop? History? Importance? Use/abuse?

Date — Event

6000 B.C.E. — Tobacco began growing in _Americas_
same family as _the poteitor_

1 B.C.E. — _Report in Indians_

417-618 — Maya & Toltec Indians spread/ borrowed tobacco customs
Higher rocky

1492 — Christopher Columbus: _came into the americas_
recieve tobacco as a gift
Tobacco introduction to world:

1556 — France

1558 — Portugal

1565 — England

1580 — Turkey

1590 — Japan, then Korea

1612 — Virginia: John Rolfe: _Jhon Roul_

1614 — King Philip III of _Spain_:
Seville _as a tobacco center_

1615 — King James I of _America_: _import to tobacco_
England

1625 — Tobacco, colony's largest export!
Why tobacco popular? _Because it_
makes relax

Some backlash:

e.g. _____

<u>1776</u>   Tobacco's importance: American Revolution:

cautivation and social,

direct ~~tero~~ source. More than ~~money~~

very powerful.

Slave demand ↑

Why? _Keeping down_

Types of tobacco use

cigarettes,

_____

Recognition of adverse effects & reactions

_____

_____

<u>Current</u>
<u>Tobacco</u>
<u>Statistics</u>

• _over million_ smokers in world. If trend continues →
  _1.86 b_ by _2025_
• _5 hundred million_ people alive now will be killed by tobac.
• Smoke-related diseases responsible for _1 in 10 dut_
• developing countries: _80% livir in de_ ~~2/3~~
  ◦ By 2030, _50% today_
• Highest cig. consumption & production : _China_
• daily _18 - 100.000_ youth addicted to tobac.

STUDY STRATEGY

Review key ideas from your notes in a study group to improve learning. Work in groups of three and ask each other about key points brought up in the lecture (e.g., "Why was tobacco so important during the American Revolution?").

ACTIVITY **4**   **REPLAY QUESTION**

🎧 **Listen to a section of the lecture. Then answer the question. Check (✓) the correct answer.**

Why does the professor read something written by a nineteenth-century historian?

____ **a.** It shows evidence that tobacco was truly important at the time.

____ **b.** It compares the importance of tobacco to other crops of the time.

____ **c.** It presents an opinion that is different from the professor's own opinion.

____ **d.** It is a digression (off the topic and unrelated to what he is lecturing about).

A student from China visited the professor during an office hour. Listen to their conversation and check (✓) the answer to each question below.

1. Why does the student want to talk to the professor?

____ a. She is concerned about missing some homework and wants to know how to make it up.

____ b. She is concerned about missing some information in class because her English is not good enough and she wants to know what to do about it.

____ c. She feels completely confused in the class and doesn't feel that she can talk to her classmates easily because of their different cultures.

____ d. She is concerned about missing some information in class because she doesn't have the expected cultural and historical knowledge.

2. What does the professor suggest to the student?

____ a. That she get a tutor to help her with the class material

____ b. That she get a textbook or check a Web site to learn more about U.S. history

____ c. That she join some clubs so she can meet other students and learn more about U.S. culture

____ d. That she drop the class and re-enroll when her English improves

3. What can be inferred about the professor's attitude toward the student's work?

____ a. He thinks she is lazy and hasn't studied enough.

____ b. He thinks that most students in her situation would not have her kinds of problems.

____ c. He understands her situation but wants her to take action to remedy it.

____ d. He thinks her problem cannot be solved.

4. In the United States, professors have scheduled office hours at which time students can typically "drop in." It is often possible to make appointments at other times if necessary. Write three reasons why students would meet with a professor outside of class.

a. _____

b. _____

c. _____

Use your notes to answer the following questions.

1. Match the reason with the result:

____ 1. Because he wanted Spain to control the distribution and production of tobacco,

____ 2. Because of the pressure to produce more and more on tobacco plantations,

____ 3. Because the Mayan Indians moved from their original locations,

____ 4. Because tobacco was so important during the Revolutionary War,

____ 5. Because he wanted England to benefit from tobacco production in the colonies,

a. King James I made tobacco imports a royal monopoly.

b. customs and rituals for tobacco use spread in the Americas.

c. a tobacco leaf was printed on money at that time.

d. King Philip III said that all tobacco imported from the Spanish New World had to come through Seville.

e. the demand for slave labor grew in the American south.

2. You will hear eight statements about the lecture. Use your notes to decide whether each statement is true or false. Write *T* or *F*.

a. ____   c. ____   e. ____   g. ____

b. ____   d. ____   f. ____   h. ____

3. Write six statements about the information in the lecture. Include both true and false statements. Read them to your classmates and have them say whether each statement is true or false.

a. _____

b. _____

c. _____

d. _____

e. _____

f. _____

ACTIVITY 7 **COMPARING IDEAS**

Compare with your classmates your answers to the preceding questions. If you have different answers, check your notes and discuss your reasons for making your choices.

Discuss the following questions in small groups.

1. Think about a country that you are familiar with. What crops grow or have been grown in that country? What do you know about the history of those particular crops? (When did cultivation start? Who did the labor? What political, economic, social, or psychological effects resulted from this crop's cultivation?)

2. Can you think of other crops that, like tobacco, have influenced social and economic and political history globally?

3. The health risks involved with tobacco use are now well known. However, tobacco use is increasing, especially in developing countries. How do you explain this? Do you agree with efforts to ban advertising and limit tobacco use?

ACTIVITY 9 **ACADEMIC WORD LIST VOCABULARY**

Match the word and its meaning. Write the correct letter in the space provided. (An example is given to help you see the word in context.)

Group 1
  a. to aim at; to choose as a focus (for work or change)
  b. to provide money for; to fund
  c. to adjust; to change so something functions in a different way
  d. to forbid; to not allow; to ban
  e. to create; to set up; to found

____ 1. *adapt*   They adapted their farming techniques when they moved to drier climates.

____ 2. *prohibit*   Laws prohibited smoking on planes years ago.

____ 3. *target*   Tobacco companies are still targeting young people in their ads.

____ 4. *establish*   They established the business in 1920.

____ 5. *finance*   In order to finance the business, they got a loan from the bank.

Group 2
  a. formal papers
  b. a general word for items that can be sold
  c. a general pattern or fashion
  d. a system organized from higher to lower by status or function
  e. the process of eating, drinking, or using something

	6. *commodity*	Gold is a precious commodity.
	7. *documents*	Keep important documents such as insurance papers in a safe place.
	8. *hierarchy*	In most large corporations, there is a hierarchy with a CEO (chief executive officer) on top.
	9. *consumption*	The consumption of tobacco products is increasing in developing countries.
	10. *trend*	We've seen a trend toward increased consumption of organic foods.

Group 3
- a. conscious of; knowledgeable about
- b. possible
- c. unimportant
- d. very big; huge; gigantic
- e. intricate; having many parts or details

	11. *enormous*	The Mayan Indians built enormous pyramids.
	12. *aware*	The farmers weren't aware of safer insecticides.
	13. *complex*	The Mayans had a complex social system.
	14. *potential*	Investors consider buying land for its potential value even if it is worthless at the time.
	15. *minor*	The Mayans had a great deal of influence—not a minor influence— on neighboring groups.

ACTIVITY 10 **USING VOCABULARY**

Read the following conversation between a former and current smoker. Fill in the blanks with vocabulary below. Use each word only once.

> *addicted*   *attitude**   *relax**   *despite**   *ritual*

A: I gave up smoking five years ago. I don't know how you can continue smoking _____ all the health warnings.

B: I know. I'm clearly _____ to smoking.

A: I remember that I didn't think I could _____ without a cigarette. It was part of my morning _____ : I'd get up, have a cup of coffee and my first cigarette. I really liked that. I had to change my _____ before I could change my habits. But I did. And I feel like a new person.

 Listen to the conversation to check your answers.

Write at least five words from this lecture unit that you would like to be able to use in speaking or writing. Write a question using that word and then ask your classmates your questions.

Example

orchard: Have you ever been in an apple orchard?

1. _____

_____

2. _____

_____

3. _____

_____

4. _____

_____

5. _____

_____

VOCABULARY LEARNING STRATEGY

Learners can understand more vocabulary than they can use. Active vocabulary learners decide which words are important for production—not just reception—and practice those words in written and/or spoken contexts.

ACTIVITY **12** **BEYOND THE LECTURE: WRITING**

Complete one of these assignments.

1. Write a paragraph about a crop or food item whose history you know.

2. Research a crop or food item and write a paragraph about key points in its history.

3. Write a "creation" story or legend for a crop or food item. Be imaginative! (For example, Who invented pizza and why? How did it happen? Why do grapes grow on a vine? Why are tomatoes red?)

FOCUS ON LECTURE ORGANIZATION

(PART 1)

Goals

- Understand the importance of recognizing lecture organization plans
- Learn about and recognize three organizational plans used by lecturers: defining a term, listing subtopics, and describing a causal relationship
- Learn about the cues that signal these organizational plans
- Listen to and take notes on lectures using these organizational plans
- Practice using notes to answer various test-type questions
- Expand academic and subject-specific vocabulary

DISCUSSION

Organization

1. How organized are you on a scale from 1 (*very disorganized*) to 6 (*very organized*)? Consider how you organize such things as closets, drawers, bookshelves, paperwork, music, desktops, storage space, computer files, bills, appointments, school projects, and so on. Why do you rate yourself as you do?

2. What is the value of being organized?

3. Two different people may be organized but have different styles of organization. Compare your organizing style with your classmates' styles.

A Why Listen for Organization?

When listening to a lecture, the listener should first try to identify the lecturer's goals. For example, does the lecturer want the listener to

- learn a definition?
- visualize how something looks?
- understand how something works?
- understand a concept?

Generally, a lecturer organizes his or her ideas in some manner in order to communicate them. Although lecturers vary in the extent to which they follow an outline, even lecturers who talk "off the top of their head" have an organizational plan and goals.

Research has shown that it is easier to remember interrelated information than isolated facts. By recognizing the organization of a lecture, the listener is better able to relate facts to each other. Specifically, the listener is better able to

- understand the lecturer's goals
- make predictions about where the lecture is heading
- retain information

B Organizational Plans within Lectures

Remember Rule 7 of the DOs and DON'Ts for improving lecture comprehension and note-taking in Unit 4:

> **DON'T** lose sight of the forest for the trees. (Don't listen for details before getting the larger picture.)
>
> **DO** listen for the lecturer's main points and for the general organizational framework.

Organization occurs on many different levels of a lecture. For example, the purpose of the lecture as a whole may be to show the cause-and-effect relationship between two events or to describe a process. That would be the general organizational framework of the lecture.

Organization is also present *within* the lecture. For example, the lecturer's main goal may be to make a generalization and support that generalization. However, in order to do that, the lecturer may define terms, provide examples, or describe processes. Consider this example: A lecturer states that "there has been much research on the effects of smoke from a nuclear explosion" and follows this with a description of the research that has been done on this topic from 1980 to the present. This lecturer would then be using two organizational plans: (a) making a generalization and providing evidence and (b) describing a sequence of events.

How does a listener recognize these organizational plans? Three plans are examined in more detail in this unit:

- defining a term
- listing subtopics
- describing a causal relationship

Other plans are examined in later chapters.

Defining a Term

Sometimes a lecturer's goal is to define a term. A **simple definition** can take the form of a single statement, such as "The biosphere is simply that region of the earth in which organisms can exist." An **extended definition** expands on the ideas in the simple definition by explaining the term in more detail. An extended definition might even be a whole lecture!

Notes from a lecture using this pattern might look like this:

> Biosphere — region of earth in which organisms can exist
>   — extends ↑ to ~20,000 ft. altitude
>   —   "   ↓ to bottom of ocean
>   —   "   inwards to limit of 100 ft.

When the lecturer gives a definition, the listener's task is to note the key words or the ideas that make up the definition.

CUES TO RECOGNIZE SIMPLE AND EXTENDED DEFINITIONS

1. Rhetorical questions that refer back to a term:

   What do I mean by X?

   How can we define X?

2. Words or phrases that signal a definition or explanation:

   (Now,) X means (is the word for) . . .

   By X, I mean (meant, referred to) . . .

   When I used X, I meant (was referring to) . . .

   In other words, . . .

   Or . . . , to use another term . . .

3. Terms that are written on the board and explained:

biotic:

4. Terms that are followed by appositives (noun phrase definitions):

   These are the biotic components . . . the living components . . .

5. Stress, intonation, and pauses used with appositives:

   These are the biotic components . . . the living components . . .

   Note the stress on the words *biotic* and *living*, which emphasize their importance. Note the pause between *biotic components* and *the living components*. Finally, note the repetition of the stress pattern for *the biotic components* and *the living components*. All of the paralinguistic features of language (stress, intonation, pauses) carry meaning.

Exercise 1

Listen for the appositive in each of the following excerpts. Write the meaning of each word.

> *Example*
> abiotic: <u>nonbiological</u>

1. *herbivores:* <u>eat or plant eaters</u>

2. *terminology:* <u>vocabulary of work</u>

3. *kin:* <u>family group</u>

Exercise 2

Listen to each of the following lecture excerpts. While listening, write the definition of each term.

> *Example*
> In this excerpt from a psychology lecture, the lecturer defines what he means by *moral development.*
>
> *moral development:* <u>what's reasoning behind why u choose to do sth or NOT?</u>

1. In this excerpt from a lecture on family systems, the lecturer defines two contrasting terms.

   a. *exogamy* _marriage outside the family group_

   b. *endogamy* _the person who marriage inside the family_

2. In this excerpt, also from a lecture on family systems, the lecturer again defines two contrasting terms.

   a. *emic* _poin of view inside in the culture_

   b. *etic* _point of view outside the culture_

3. In this excerpt from a lecture on psychology, the lecturer defines *egocentrism*:

   egocentrism: _my way it's my only way._

Listing Subtopics

In some cases, the lecturer's goal is to break a topic down by listing or enumerating a number of its features. For example, in a lecture on Amnesty International, a human rights organization, the lecturer lists eight principles on which the group's work is based.

Notes from this lecture might look like this:

> 8 Principles Underlying Amnesty International's Work
> 1. limited field of authority
>   — limits work to political imprisonment, torture, execution
> 2. focus on individual prisoner
>   — does not work in abstract
>   — seeks contact w/ prisoners & families
> 3. all action is grounded in fact
>   — reliable info. essential
>   — conducts fact-finding missions

Note that each numbered item is related to the larger heading in the same way as the other numbered items. In other words, they are all underlying principles of Amnesty International's work. To show this, the numbered items are indented equally.

CUES TO RECOGNIZE LISTS

1. Numbers that indicate listed items:

   The first (second, third) point is . . .
   Number one (two, three) . . .
   First (second, third) . . .

2. Stress that emphasizes numbers:

   The first principle is . . .

3. Phrases or sentences that signal a list of forthcoming items:

   There are eight principles that underlie Amnesty International's work.
   Stress can be reduced in a number of ways.

Exercise 3

 You will hear three lecture excerpts that list information. First, read the information about each excerpt. Then, while listening to the excerpt, take notes in the spaces provided.

Example
Excerpt from a lecture on psychology

How did researchers judge psych. distress?

Heading — 5 measures:

List —
1. How much anxiety?
2. "   "   irritability?
3. "   "   somatic (bodily) complaints?
4. "   "   depression?
5. "   "   difficulty w/ thinking & concentrating?

1. Excerpt from a lecture on ecology

   Vocabulary

   ecosystem: a system involving a relationship between organisms and the
       environment
   nutrient: an ingredient in food that nourishes (i.e., keeps an organism alive)

Heading

List

> Essential Abiotic Factors for Life in Ecosystem—
>
> 1. Temperature
> 2. Nutrients
> 3. Lied
> 4. Moisture

2. Excerpt from a lecture on eight steps of topic analysis for library research

Heading

List

> While Surveying Topic & Clarifying Terms
> 1. Explain pictures
> 2. B. Terminology of the vocabulary of the topic

3. Excerpt from a lecture on memory

VOCABULARY

mental faculties: mental powers

Heading

List

> How to remember? Where are mental faculties (incl. learning, memory)?
>
> 1. head (since early 19th c.)
> 2. Greeks
> 3. Egyptians

 E Describing a Causal Relationship

Sometimes the lecturer's goal is to describe a relationship between events in which one event leads to (or may or should lead to) one or more events.

This pattern might include a combination of the following:

- a description of a problem or the circumstances surrounding an event
- the causes of, or reasons for, the problem or circumstances
- the effects of the problem or circumstances
- the solutions to a problem

Notes from a lecture using this pattern might look like this:

Acid rain
    — destroys structures
    — harms environment
Causes?
    — auto emissions
    — industrial emissions

CUES TO RECOGNIZE CAUSAL RELATIONSHIPS

1. Words and phrases that signal a causal relationship:

    Due to the fact that . . .
    Because (of) . . .
    Since . . .
    Conditional sentences: If . . . , (then) . . .
    (Now) this is due to . . .
    It has nothing to do with X, but rather . . .
    . . . and the reason for this is . . .

2. Words or phrases that signal the effect of a previously stated event:

    Thus, . . .
    Therefore, . . .
    Consequently, . . .
    For these reasons . . .
    We can draw some conclusions . . .

3. Rhetorical questions that signal a discussion of the cause of a previously stated event:

    How can we explain this?
    How did we get to this point?
    Why is this the case?

4. Rhetorical questions that signal a discussion of the solution to a previously stated problem:

    What can be done about this?
    How can we solve this?
    What can we do?

Exercise 4

 You will hear three lecture excerpts that describe causal relationships. First, read the information about each excerpt. Then, while listening, take notes in the spaces provided.

Example

Excerpt from a lecture on marriage and divorce trends in the United States

Event | 1940 — Close to begin of WW II (Pre-War)

↓

Effect | People get married quicker

↑ # of people marrying

Cause | Why? ♂ to war, want marry 1st

1. Excerpt from a lecture on marriage and divorce trends in the United States

Event | 1945 — Men come home fr. war

↓

Effect | marriage rate = as 1940   12.2 per 1k

divorce increase   from 1940   3.5 per 1k

Cause | Why? " out of sight , out of mind "

" absence makes the heart grow fonder "

2. Excerpt from a lecture on evolutionary psychology

VOCABULARY

maturity: the quality of behaving in a sensible way and like an adult
resources: the money, property, skills, etc. that one has available for use

Result | Why ♀ want ♂ slightly older?

Resource Argument

Cause | — More time to amass resources

3. Excerpt from a lecture on acid rain

Problem | Acid rain ↑ w/industrialization

Solution | Solutions? Put controlls , not polluting . create a tchnology

to reduce it

Problem w/ solution | BUT cost much money .

How to Deal with Stress   (Psychology)

Vocabulary

Related to Stress

Check (✓) the words you know. Underline the words you want to learn. Then check their meaning with your instructor or in a dictionary.

stress
tension
anxiety
irritability

stressed
tense
anxious
irritable

cope

stressors
sources of stress

Signs of stress

insomnia
shortness/tightness of
  breath
accelerated breathing
muscle spasm
nervous tic
high blood pressure

When I feel stressed, I tend to eat more. Then I feel worse!

When I get stressed, I become irritable. It drives my family crazy.

Stress gives me insomnia.

When I get stressed, I just want to crawl into bed and sleep, sleep, sleep!

Whenever I feel stressed, I force myself to take a short, brisk walk.

ACTIVITY **1** **PRE-LECTURE READING AND DISCUSSION**

The following scale was developed by Dr. Thomas Holmes and Dr. Richard Rahe in their research on how stress affects health.

Try the scale for yourself. Give yourself the indicated points for each life event that you have experienced in the past year. Then discuss your answers to the questions that follow.

THE SOCIAL READJUSTMENT RATING SCALE

Life Event	Mean Value
1. Death of spouse	100
2. Divorce	73
3. Marital separation from mate	65
4. Detention in jail or other institution	63
5. Death of a close family member	63
6. Major personal injury or illness	53
7. Marriage	50
8. Being fired at work	47
9. Marital reconciliation with mate	45
10. Retirement from work	45
11. Major change in the health or behavior of a family member	44
12. Pregnancy	40
13. Sexual difficulties	39
14. Gaining a new family member (e.g., through birth, adoption, elder moving in)	39
15. Major business readjustment (e.g., merger, reorganization, bankruptcy)	39
16. Major change in financial state (i.e., much worse or better off than usual)	38
17. Death of a close friend	37
18. Changing to a different line of work	36
19. Major change in the number of arguments with spouse (i.e., much more or less than usual)	35
20. Taking out a mortgage or loan for a major purchase (e.g., for a home or business)	31
21. Foreclosure on a mortgage or loan	30
22. Major change in responsibilities at work (e.g., promotion, demotion, or lateral transfer)	29
23. Son or daughter leaving home (e.g., for marriage or college)	29
24. Trouble with in-laws	29
25. Outstanding personal achievement	28
26. Spouse beginning or ceasing work outside the home	26
27. Beginning or ceasing formal schooling	26

(continued on next page)

28. Major change in living conditions (e.g., building a new home, remodeling, or deterioration of home or neighborhood)............. 25

29. Revision of personal habits (e.g., dress, manners, or associations) 24

30. Trouble with the boss 23

31. Major change in working hours or conditions............................. 20

32. Change in residence... 20

33. Changing to a new school 20

34. Major change in usual type and/or amount of recreation............ 19

35. Major change in church/temple activities (i.e., attending much more or less than usual)... 19

36. Major change in social activities (e.g., clubs, movies, or visiting)... 18

37. Taking out a mortgage or loan for a lesser purchase (e.g., for a car, TV, or freezer)... 17

38. Major change in sleeping habits (e.g., much more or less sleep, or change in part of day when asleep).. 16

39. Major change in number of family get-togethers (e.g., much more or less than usual) 15

40. Major change in eating habits (e.g., much more or less food intake, or very different meal hours or surroundings).......... 15

41. Vacation 13

42. Christmas.. 12

43. Minor violations of the law (e.g., traffic tickets, jaywalking, or disturbing the peace)... 11

1. What is your "stress score"? How does your score compare with your classmates' scores?

2. According to this scale, is stress always caused by unpleasant events?

3. Would this scale be appropriate for all ages? If not, how might it differ for adolescents? older teens? Would this scale be appropriate for all cultures? If not, why not?

4. In their study, Dr. Holmes and Dr. Rahe found that 79 percent of those who scored more than 300 points on this scale developed a major illness within the year that followed. Do you think this proves that stress causes illness? Why or why not?

5. Do you think that your stress score is too high? What steps can people take to reduce the effects of stress on the body?

PREPARING FOR THE LECTURE

The title of the lecture is "How to Deal with Stress." What do you expect the lecturer to tell you about this? Brainstorm ideas with your classmates.

🎧 **Listen to the introduction. Then answer the questions.**

1. What will the lecturer talk about? Check (✓) one or more answers.
   - ✓ **a.** What stress is
   - ____ **b.** Who has the most stress
   - ✓ **c.** How to cope with stress
   - ____ **d.** How to live without stress

2. What will come next?
   - ____ **a.** A list of things that cause stress
   - ____ **b.** A list of ways to cope with stress
   - ✓ **c.** A definition of stress
   - ____ **d.** Some causes of stress

ACTIVITY **3** **LISTENING FOR THE LARGER PICTURE**

🎧 **Read the following summaries before the lecture begins. Then, listen to the lecture once without taking notes. After listening, check (✓) the letter of the summary that most closely describes the lecture.**

____ **a.** The lecturer primarily compares the two types of stress: negative stress and positive stress. Then, she lists ways to deal with negative stress.

____ **b.** The lecturer primarily talks about the health hazards associated with stress and lists the reasons why people should avoid stress.

____ **c.** The lecturer defines stress and talks about two types of stress. Then, the lecturer focuses on the main part of the talk, which involves a list of ways that one can deal with stress appropriately.

____ **d.** The lecturer states that stress is hazardous in itself and then provides evidence for that generalization. Finally, the lecturer lists ways to eliminate stress from one's life.

Did you know?

Cuts and wounds heal more slowly and people are more likely to get an infection if they're under a lot of stress.

ACTIVITY **4** **ORGANIZATION**

Read this summary of the lecture organization.

> The lecture primarily demonstrates two organizational plans: **defining a term** and **listing subtopics**. The lecturer begins by defining stress, giving a simple definition, and then expanding that definition with additional details. The lecturer then lists five ways to deal with stress appropriately, giving examples or additional details about each way as needed.

Do you remember anything about the lecturer's definition of stress? Do you remember anything about any of the five ways to deal with stress? Discuss with a partner.

The following words and expressions were used in the lecture that you just heard. You may remember the contexts in which you heard them.

You will now hear an additional example of each word or expression in a new context. After listening, check (✓) the letter of the definition that most closely matches what you think the word or expression means.

1. *virtually**
   - ✓ **a.** rarely; almost never the case
   - ___ **b.** more or less true in practical terms
   - ___ **c.** ideally; as it would be in the ideal world

2. *immune*
   - ✓ **a.** unaffected; invulnerable
   - ___ **b.** affected; vulnerable
   - ___ **c.** sickly; ill

3. *adapt*
   - ___ **a.** to take for one's own
   - ___ **b.** to raise another person's child
   - ✓ **c.** to adjust for a particular use

4. *hazardous*
   - ✓ **a.** unpleasant
   - ___ **b.** unusual
   - ✓ **c.** dangerous

5. *monitor**
   - ✓ **a.** to protect
   - ✓ **b.** to check regularly
   - ___ **c.** to harm or damage

6. *regardless of*
   - ✓ **a.** in spite of; without concern about
   - ___ **b.** because of; due to
   - ___ **c.** next to; adjacent to

7. *out of one's hands*
   - ___ **a.** not in one's interest
   - ___ **b.** not in one's sight
   - ✓ **c.** not in one's power

8. *inevitable**
   - ___ **a.** unable to be considered
   - ___ **b.** unable to be enjoyed
   - ✓ **c.** unable to be avoided or prevented

9. *pace*
   - ✓ **a.** to adjust the speed or timing
   - ___ **b.** to run a long-distance competition
   - ___ **a.** to receive a prize

Did you know?

When dog or cat owners were asked to solve a difficult mathematical problem, they showed less stress in the company of their pets than in the company of a friend.

Listen to the lecture a second time. Take notes using the following format.
The comments in the left margin show the organization of the lecture.

Introduction

Definition of
stress

What is stress? discrite the force between two bodies.
Huma body reaction. Body's non response, Muscle tension

pleasent or not. Positive or negative.

Types of stress
and examples

- Positive way (Christmas) (marciage)
- Negative feels negative (friends' death)

Ways to cope with
stress

Ways to deal w/stress appropriately:

1. To recogrize your stress signals. To
focus on minimezing. (smoking)

2. To pay attentions to your bodies
denands.

3. Make plans withe the appropiate
people. Reduce the stress secause reduce
the worry.

4. To learn to controled the
situation. Learn except the things in your
head

5. To pays your activities

Conclusion

Bring your test. Only 24h in a day
So you have many time to do different
things.

Listen to a section of the lecture. Then answer the questions.

1. Why does the lecturer talk about writing a term paper? Check (✓) one.

   ____ a. To give details about the next class assignment

   ____ b. To give an example about pacing one's activities

   ____ c. To compare and contrast different ways of handling difficult assignments

   ____ d. To show how term papers cause students stress

2. What does the lecturer mean by "Why don't we open the floor to comments?"

LISTENING AND NOTE-TAKING STRATEGIES

1. Review your notes as soon as possible after listening. Perhaps there was information that you heard but did not have time to note. Add information that you remember.

2. Ask classmates for specific pieces of information that you might have missed. ("I didn't catch the last suggestion for dealing with stress. Did you get that?" "I'm not sure I got the definition of stress correctly. Can I see your notes for a second?")

3. Consider rewriting your notes soon after listening. You can make the relationship between ideas clearer by indenting or using headings, for example.

ACTIVITY 8 "OTHER VOICES" FOLLOW-UP

Two students are talking about the lecture afterwards. Listen to their conversation. Then answer the question. Check (✓) the correct answer.

Which of the following is *not* mentioned by one of the students?

____ a. A feeling of being overwhelmed

____ b. An opinion about what was missing from the lecture

____ c. An interest in learning more about the subject

____ d. A belief that it's important to prioritize activities

ACTIVITY 9 POST-LECTURE DISCUSSION

Discuss your answers to the following questions in small groups.

1. The lecturer's first suggestion for dealing with stress appropriately is to recognize your own stress signals. The lecturer mentions that people have different early signs of stress. What are *your* early stress signals?

2. What do you think the following quote means?

I remember the story of the old man who said on his deathbed that he had had a lot of trouble in his life—most of which never happened.

—Winston Churchill, British Prime Minister (1874–1965)

How does this idea relate to your own life?

3. Talk about a stressful time in your life. What did you do (and/or what could you have done) to manage the stress better?

ACTIVITY 10 **USING YOUR NOTES**

Use your notes to answer the following questions.

1. According to this lecture, stress is the body's

____ **a.** nonspecific response to any unpleasant demand placed on it

____ **b.** specific response to any unpleasant demand placed on it

____ **c.** nonspecific response to any demand placed on it, pleasant or unpleasant

____ **d.** specific response to any demand placed on it, pleasant or unpleasant

2. In what field of study did the term *stress* originate?

_____

3. What is *eustress*?

_____

4. The lecturer lists five ways to deal with stress appropriately. What are they?

a. _____

b. _____

c. _____

d. _____

e. _____

5. True or false?

____ Stress, in itself, is hazardous.

6. What is the lecturer's attitude about stress?

____ **a.** It is important to avoid stress because it is always harmful.

____ **b.** It is important to manage stress well.

____ **c.** People who do not have stress are lucky.

____ **d.** People who manage stress well are lucky.

1. In small groups, compare your answers to the preceding questions. If you have different answers, check your notes and discuss your reasons for making your choices.

2. Compare your rewritten notes to the sample rewritten notes in Appendix D. Notice the organization. Is yours similar or different? Are your notes equally effective in making important ideas stand out?

ACTIVITY **12** **ACADEMIC WORD LIST VOCABULARY**

Fill in the chart with the missing forms. Then choose one of the words in the chart to complete the sentences below. The meaning of the word you need is in parentheses. Change verb forms as needed.

VERB	NOUN
achieve	
acknowledge	
	adaptation
	minimization
	occurrence
respond	
benefit	

1. I wish he had (recognized) _____ all the work I'd done.

2. There was no (answer) _____ to my question.

3. He is proud of all that he has (successfully done) _____.

4. Her work (does good for) _____ society.

5. Don't (underestimate) _____ the work you have done; everyone can see that you've done a lot!

6. Our goal is to reduce the (event) _____ of health problems.

7. (Adjustment to a new situation) _____ is necessary if animals are going to survive in new environments.

You will hear vocabulary from the lecture in different contexts. Listen before reading each exercise. After listening, check (✓) the letter of the sentence that most closely paraphrases the information that you heard.

What a Night!

1. ____ a. He slept well last night.
   ____ b. He slept poorly last night.
   ____ c. He didn't sleep at all last night.

2. ____ a. He is easily annoyed because he doesn't sleep well.
   ____ b. He doesn't sleep well because he is easily annoyed by things that happen to him.
   ____ c. He is in a wonderful mood because of his good night's sleep.

3. ____ a. His wife is not affected by the noise outside the window.
   ____ b. His wife is somewhat affected by the noise.
   ____ c. His wife is greatly affected by the noise.

4. ____ a. Traffic speeds by at certain hours of the night.
   ____ b. Traffic rarely speeds by at night.
   ____ c. Traffic speeds by at all hours of the night.

5. ____ a. The husband is trying to solve the problem himself without complaining to the authorities.
   ____ b. The husband is gathering evidence before he complains to the authorities.
   ____ c. The husband is changing his behavior so he can get used to the situation instead of complaining.

Burnout

1. ____ a. People who have been physically injured tend to have difficulties handling the stress in all or part of their lives.
   ____ b. People who experience burnout have a hard time dealing with all or part of their lives.

2. ____ a. According to psychologists, people who don't know how to manage their time and energy will probably experience burnout.
   ____ b. Burnout may prevent people from pacing themselves.

ACTIVITY 14 RETAINING VOCABULARY

VOCABULARY LEARNING STRATEGY

Create flash cards to help you remember new words and their definitions. Review them regularly. On the front of the card, write the word. On the back, write the definition or draw a picture that defines the word. (If you found the word in a complete sentence or your dictionary gives an example sentence, it is helpful to copy that sentence too, as it gives you a context for how the word is used.)

Choose ten words from the lecture, reading, or discussion that you would like to remember. Write them here:

1. _____   6. _____

2. _____   7. _____

3. _____   8. _____

4. _____   9. _____

5. _____   10. _____

Then create flashcards. On the front of the card, write the word. On the back, draw a picture that suggests the word or write a definition. Exchange your flashcards with a partner and quiz each other.

ACTIVITY 15 BEYOND THE LECTURE: WRITING, SPEAKING, LISTENING, RESEARCHING

Complete one of these assignments.

1. Write about a stressful event or time in your life and what you did to manage the stress then. Discuss whether the lecturer's suggestions for coping with stress were relevant in your situation. Could the lecturer's suggestions or any other techniques have helped you handle the stress better or differently?

2. Surf the Web to find helpful sites on stress reduction. Here are some search terms to consider: "stress management," "stress reduction," "coping with stress." Be skeptical when exploring sites that are selling products; although they may offer some helpful information, their primary goal is to get you to buy something. Instead, look for sites that are produced and maintained by nonprofit organizations such as professional organizations, educational institutions, and government agencies.

Be prepared to speak to classmates about three sites you visited, why you recommend or don't recommend those sites, and what additional information you learned about stress management from them.

Use the form below to gather your thoughts.

Site address	Who "owns" the site? Is it maintained by • a governmental, educational, or nonprofit institution? • a business? • an individual? What is the creator's goal in setting up this site?	What additional information did you learn about stress and stress management from this site?	Do you recommend this site? Why or why not?

Acid Rain (Ecology/Chemistry)

Vocabulary

Related to Pollution

Check (✓) the words you know. Underline the words you want to learn. Then check their meaning with your instructor or in a dictionary.

hazardous
toxic

haze
smog

emit
discharge

fumes
emissions
waste (products)
pollutants

contaminate
corrode

dispose of

natural resource

environment
ecology

recycle

curb
cut down on

ACTIVITY **1** **PRE-LECTURE READING AND DISCUSSION**

Read the following excerpt from a magazine article about acid rain. When you are finished, discuss your answers to the questions that follow in small groups.

The International Acid Test

ANNE LaBASTILLE, *Sierra* Magazine

My log cabin looks out over a lake that has grown increasingly clear in recent years, with a strange layer of algae spreading across the bottom. Native trout are now scarce, as are certain types of fish-eating birds. Bullfrogs are few and far between. As much as a third of the virgin red spruce around the lake have died.

When I dropped a pH meter in the lake right after the snowmelt in 1985, it measured a very acidic 3.9. In the summer of 1979, it had measured 4.3, and in 1933, according to state records, it was a healthy 6.3.

I've noticed these and many other changes in the twenty years I've lived in the Adirondack Mountains of upstate New York, one of the regions hardest hit by acid rain. Many of my neighbors have had to replace their copper and lead plumbing with plastic lines as acidic waters corroded the pipes. At least 600 lakes and ponds in the Western Adirondacks have been acidified to some degree, and the red spruce forests on the higher peaks show extensive damage.

After studying the problems with acid rain in this country, I traveled to Scandinavia and Switzerland to take a look at the big picture. This foreign exposure revealed that acid fallout is not just an American or Canadian problem; it affects Europe and all densely populated, industrialized nations that use fossil fuels to produce energy.

Acid rain is also threatening trout high in the Rocky Mountains and sugar maples in Vermont and Ontario. It is dissolving India's Taj Mahal and is making some European game animals' organs unfit to eat. According to Earthscan, an independent news service, more than 16 million acres of forest in nine European countries have been damaged by acid rain. The Acropolis, the Tower of London, and Cologne Cathedral are also becoming victims. As one Danish architect commented, "These buildings are melting away like sugar candy." Even urban areas of Latin America and Africa are showing signs of damage.

1. LaBastille lists a number of effects of acid rain on the area around her home in the Adirondack Mountains, as well as effects of acid rain worldwide. What are those effects?

2. Had you heard of acid rain before reading this article? What do you know about it? Share your knowledge with your group.

3. Though this article was written more than twenty years ago, acid rain is still an issue today. The problems still exist even though international organizations and individual nations have signed treaties and created programs to control the emissions that result in acid rain. What do you know about any treaties that have been signed or programs that have been created? Why do you think the problems still have not been solved?

Did you know?

Acid "rain" isn't just rain; acid snow, acid fog or mist, acid gas, and acid dust all have the same effect as acid rain.

ACTIVITY ② **PREPARING FOR THE LECTURE**

The title of the lecture is "Acid Rain." What about acid rain do you expect the lecturer to tell you? Brainstorm ideas with your classmates.

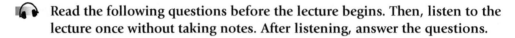 **Listen to the beginning of the lecture. Then answer the question.**

What will come next? Check (✓) one.

_____ **a.** A list of different types of pollution

_____ **b.** Statistics about acid rain in different countries

_____ **c.** A definition of acid rain

_____ **d.** Examples of ways people can reduce acid rain

ACTIVITY ③ **LISTENING FOR THE LARGER PICTURE**

Read the following questions before the lecture begins. Then, listen to the lecture once without taking notes. After listening, answer the questions.

1. The lecturer begins the talk by stating a number of surprising facts and statistics about acid rain. Why would a lecturer choose to begin in this way?

   _____.

2. The lecturer's goal is to tell the audience about acid rain. In order to do this, which of the following does he do? Check (✓) all correct answers.

   _____ **a.** Classifies the types of acid rain

   _____ **b.** Defines acid rain

   _____ **c.** Gives the causes of acid rain

   _____ **d.** Gives the effects of acid rain

   _____ **e.** Presents solutions to the problem of acid rain

   _____ **f.** Compares and contrasts acid rain to other forms of pollution

ACTIVITY ④ **ORGANIZATION**

Read this summary of the lecture organization.

The lecture primarily demonstrates two organizational plans: **giving a definition** and **describing a causal relationship**.

- At the beginning, there is a simple definition of acid rain.
- The lecturer then goes into detail about that definition by, for example, comparing the pH of acid rain to that of "pure" rain.
- The lecturer later gives a number of sources (or causes) of acid rain and then gives a number of its effects.
- The lecturer ends by very briefly stating some possible solutions.

Do you remember anything about the lecturer's definition of acid rain? the sources or causes of acid rain? the effects of acid rain? the solutions to the problem? Discuss with a partner.

ACTIVITY **5** **DEFINING VOCABULARY**

The following words and expressions were used in the lecture that you just heard. You may remember the contexts in which you heard them.

You will now hear an additional example of each word or expression in a new context. After listening, check (✓) the letter of the definition that most closely matches what you think the word or expression means.

1. *corrosion*
   _____ a. the process of building with metal
   _____ b. the process of deteriorating or wearing down (especially by chemical action)
   _____ c. the process of melting (especially by applying heat)

2. *ecosystem*
   _____ a. the system that connects animals to each other
   _____ b. the system that connects plants and animals to their physical environment
   _____ c. the system that connects the economy and the environment

3. *precipitation*
   _____ a. water in any form (e.g., rain, snow, sleet) that falls on the earth
   _____ b. dry weather (e.g., the climate of the desert)
   _____ c. hot weather (e.g., the climate of regions located near the equator)

4. *source**
   _____ a. a place from which something originates
   _____ b. money
   _____ c. a flavorful liquid served over food

5. *emission*
   _____ a. something released and sent out (e.g., radiation, gas)
   _____ b. an automobile part
   _____ c. a poor driving habit

6. *vulnerable*
   _____ a. easily attacked or harmed
   _____ b. ready to attack
   _____ c. prepared for an attack

(continued on next page)

7. *predominant**

___ **a.** most powerful, important, or numerous

___ **b.** least powerful, important, or numerous

___ **c.** losing importance from the past to present

8. *level off*

___ **a.** to rise; to go up

___ **b.** to decline; to go down

___ **c.** to become steady after rising or declining

9. *adverse*

___ **a.** negative

___ **b.** positive

___ **c.** expected

10. *attribute**

___ **a.** to smoke a lot

___ **b.** to die suddenly

___ **c.** to regard as the cause

11. *toxic*

___ **a.** expensive

___ **b.** tasty

___ **c.** poisonous

12. *glacier*

___ **a.** a huge accident at sea

___ **b.** a huge mass of moving ice

___ **c.** a huge ship

13. *alternative* energy**

___ **a.** energy that comes from an atypical source (e.g., wind power)

___ **b.** energy that is caused by the decomposition of organic material (e.g., oil, gas, or coal)

___ **c.** energy that is used in large quantities

14. *airborne*

___ **a.** carried by or through the air

___ **b.** giving birth in the air

___ **c.** a fear or terror of flying

15. *eventually**

___ **a.** happening immediately

___ **b.** happening later

___ **c.** never happening

Listen to the lecture a second time. On a separate piece of paper, take notes using the following format. The comments in the left margin serve to remind you of the organization of the lecture.

Introduction	
Definition of acid rain	Acid rain
Details about definition	
Cause & effect explanation	Causes 　• Nitrogen sources 　• Sulfur sources Effects 　• On aquatic ecosystems 　• On forests 　• On architectural structures 　• On health
Conclusion	

Replay the conclusion. Then answer each question. Check (✓) the correct answer.

1. What is the lecturer's attitude about how the world is dealing with acid rain?

____ a. Very hopeful: a sufficient number of positive steps have been taken

____ b. Very hopeful: with the laws and goals that we currently have, there should be no problems in the future

____ c. Somewhat hopeful: some positive steps have been taken, but more needs to be done

____ d. Not hopeful: nothing has been done, and this will have disastrous consequences.

2. Who needs to pay attention to the problem, according to the lecturer?

____ a. The most economically developed countries

____ b. Countries with few natural resources

____ c. Europe and the Americas, in particular

____ d. Everyone in all areas

LISTENING AND NOTE-TAKING STRATEGIES

1. Review your notes as soon as possible after listening. Perhaps there was information that you heard but did not have time to note. Add information that you remember.

2. Ask classmates for specific pieces of information that you might have missed. ("The professor said that *what* percentage of nitrogen comes from *where*?")

3. Consider rewriting your notes soon after listening. You can make the relationship between ideas more clear and make important ideas stand out by indenting or using headings, for example.

ACTIVITY **8** **"OTHER VOICES" FOLLOW-UP**

After the lecture, the professor asked students to break into small groups and brainstorm ways in which they, in their personal life, could reduce their personal contribution to acid rain.

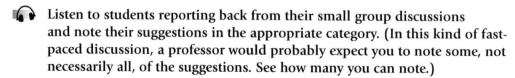 Listen to students reporting back from their small group discussions and note their suggestions in the appropriate category. (In this kind of fast-paced discussion, a professor would probably expect you to note some, not necessarily all, of the suggestions. See how many you can note.)

Did you know?

Acid rain has been linked to breathing and lung problems in children and in people who have asthma.

SUGGESTIONS RELATED TO THE HOME	SUGGESTIONS RELATED TO SHOPPING	SUGGESTIONS RELATED TO TRANSPORTATION

ACTIVITY **9** POST-LECTURE DISCUSSION

Discuss your answers to the following questions in small groups.

1. Due to increased use of fossil fuels (i.e., coal, oil, and gas) and increased industrialization, our world has become increasingly polluted. Acid rain is only one type of pollution. Do you think our industrial gains and improved standard of living outweigh the costs to our health and the environment? Justify your answer.

2. Does your lifestyle contribute to the problem of acid rain? If so, how?

3. How likely are you to make the changes in your lifestyle that the students discussed in their small groups?

ACTIVITY **10** USING YOUR NOTES

Use your notes to answer the following questions.

1. When nitrogen is released into the atmosphere, it combines with oxygen and hydrogen to become _____.

2. Fill in the charts below with information from the lecture.

SOURCE OF NITROGEN IN U.S.	%

SOURCE OF SULFUR IN U.S.	%

(continued on next page)

3. True or false?

_____ a. Acid rain refers only to rain that contains a high level of acid.

_____ b. Acid rain is particularly the United States' problem.

_____ c. Theoretically, pure rain has a pH of 1.4.

_____ d. Lakes affected by acid rain always look unhealthy.

_____ e. Trees are affected by acid rain because it destroys their roots.

_____ f. Scientists have found a direct cause/effect relationship between acid rain and human illness.

_____ g. Acid rain has always occurred at the current levels. It is only recently that we have become aware of its dangers.

ACTIVITY **11** **COMPARING IDEAS**

1. In small groups, compare your answers to the preceding questions. If you have different answers, check your notes and discuss your reasons for making your choices.

2. Compare your rewritten notes to the sample rewritten notes in Appendix D. Notice the organization. Is yours similar or different? Are your notes equally effective in making important ideas stand out?

ACTIVITY **12** **ACADEMIC WORD LIST VOCABULARY**

Fill in the chart with the noun forms. Then choose one of the words in the chart to complete the sentences on the next page. The meaning of the word you need is in parentheses.

VOCABULARY STRATEGY

Learn suffixes that change the grammatical form of words, such as *-tion*, which indicates a noun.

VERB	NOUN
generate	
dominate	
attribute	
contribute	
transport	
approximate	
alternate	

1. This is only a(n) (estimate, a general figure)_____.
   We need to do more research before we find the exact number.

2. Scientists (blame or credit as a cause) _____ the
   increase in the rate of asthma to high pollution levels.

3. We need to (move something from one place to another)
   _____ these crops from the farm to cities.

4. Each person has to consider his or her own (amount given by someone to
   an organization or effort or problem) _____ to the
   world's pollution problems.

5. The parents (move or switch back and forth) _____
   childcare responsibilities so that each one can work a few days a week.

6. I'd like to invest in your business but I don't understand how it will
   (produce) _____ a profit.

7. A few companies (have the greatest influence or power in)
   _____ the coal industry in that country.

ACTIVITY 13 **USING VOCABULARY**

**You will hear a short talk about how acid rain affected some lakes in
southern Norway. After listening, read the following summary and fill in the
blanks with words from the vocabulary list below. (You may change the verb
forms and tenses.)**

airborne	adverse effects	source*	attribute*
precipitation	ecosystem	vulnerable	toxic

The talk is about the effect of acid rain on some lakes in southern Norway. The
fish, in particular, seemed to be _____ to the acid rain. For
(1.)
example, in a 33,000 sq. km. area, there were definite _____
(2.)
on the fish population. In a 13,000 sq. km. area, all the fish died. Scientists
_____ the death of the fish to two factors: the direct
(3.)
effect of the acid and the fact that the acid rain caused aluminum from the
surrounding soil to enter the lake, killing the fish because aluminum is
_____ to fish. The death of these fish had an effect on
(4.)
the _____ of the area because animals lost an important
(5.)
_____ of food.
(6.)

VOCABULARY STRATEGY

A good way to remember a new word is to *use* it in a meaningful way.

Complete each of these statements with true information about yourself or a country that you are familiar with.

1. I *attribute* my success in _____ to _____
   because _____.

2. I feel *vulnerable* when _____
   because _____.

3. I feel most positive about _____
   as an *alternative source* of energy in _____
   because _____.

4. The *predominant* export from _____
   is _____.

5. I can't do it now, but *eventually* I hope to _____
   _____.

ACTIVITY **15** **BEYOND THE LECTURE: RESEARCHING AND PRESENTING INFORMATION**

Complete the following assignment.

Read an article from the library or the Internet about a current environmental issue (e.g., acid rain, air pollution, water pollution, the destruction of the rain forest). Prepare a five-minute presentation. Explain the main ideas of the article and conclude with your opinion and/or evaluation of these ideas. Use this outline to prepare your presentation.

Name of article:

Source of article (magazine, journal, newspaper, government Web site):

Main point(s) of article:

Your opinion/evaluation of the main point(s):

FOCUS ON LECTURE ORGANIZATION

PART 2

Goals

- Understand the importance of recognizing lecture organization plans
- Learn about and recognize three more organizational plans: exemplifying a topic, describing a process or sequence of events, and classifying
- Learn the cues that signal these organizational plans
- Listen to and take notes on lectures that use these organizational plans
- Practice using notes to answer various test-type questions
- Expand academic and subject-specific vocabulary

In Unit 6, you practiced recognizing and taking notes from lectures that used three organizational plans: defining, listing, and describing a causal relationship. In this unit, you will learn about and practice with three more plans.

DISCUSSION

Teaching and Explaining Things in Everyday Life

1. How do you learn best: by reading, by listening, by doing? Talk about something that you have taught yourself to do and how you learned.

2. It is not always easy to teach someone else how to do something that you know well. Why? Talk about a skill you taught someone else to do, for example, driving, riding a bicycle, cooking something, interviewing successfully, or playing a computer game. How did you teach this skill? In what ways were you a good teacher? Were there any ways that you could have taught the skill better?

3. Talk about a time someone tried to teach you how to do something (outside of a school situation). Was the experience easy? difficult? successful? unsuccessful? frustrating? challenging? enjoyable? What did your "teacher" do or not do that made it more or less difficult to learn?

4. How might these ideas relate to organization in lectures?

A Exemplifying a Topic

With this organizational plan, the goal of the lecturer is to clarify the topic by giving examples. For instance, in a lecture on archaeology, the lecturer talks about estimating dates by reading tree rings. He gives examples of how the rings might look under different conditions.

Notes from a lecture using this pattern might look like this:

Archaeological Dating Methods

  Tree-ring dating (dendrochronology)

   — every yr., trees grow new layer

   — create series of concentric rings

   — layer varies with climatic changes

       e.g., spring — pale ring

           drought — thin ring

   — archaeologists start from known climatic changes and

     count back

CUES TO RECOGNIZE EXAMPLES

Lecturers give examples to make an idea easier to comprehend. Sometimes they offer examples without any cues. Other times they use some of the words or phrases below.

1. Phrases that signal an example:

   For example, . . .
   For instance, . . .
   To illustrate, . . .
   In this case, . . .
   Let's say, . . .
   Take something like this . . .
   A classic example is . . .

2. Phrases or sentences that emphasize the application of a concept:

   In order to see this more clearly, . . .
   In more concrete terms, . . .
   Let's look at how this applies in the real world.

3. Rhetorical questions that signal an example:

Where can we find/see this?
How does this show up in the real world?

Exercise **1**

 You will hear three lecture excerpts that include examples. First, read the information about each excerpt. Then, while listening to the excerpt, take notes in the spaces provided.

Example
Excerpt from a lecture on memory

Heading

Examples

> *Procedural memory: memory for phys. things*
>   *e.g., bike riding, use stick shift (driving)*

1. Excerpt from a lecture on ecology

Heading

Examples

> *w/ cold-blooded animals, chem. reactions depend on temp. of environ.*
>   *e.g.*

2. Excerpt from a lecture on family systems

Heading

Examples

> *Terms for "cousin" vary in diff. languages*
>   *e.g.*

3. Excerpt from a lecture on child development

Heading

Examples

> *To communicate w/ child, do it symbolically*
>   *"animism": everything is alive for children*
>   *e.g.*

B | Describing a Process or Sequence of Events

Sometimes a lecturer's goal is to demonstrate how something happens (or has happened) by organizing information according to a process or sequence of events.

Notes from a lecture organized as a process might look like this:

> Acid Rain Process
>
> - N (nitrogen) & S (sulfur) → atmosphere
>
> - Combine with O (oxygen) and H (hydrogen)
>
> - → nitric acid (HNO_3) & sulfuric acid (H_2SO_4)

Notes from a lecture organized as a sequence of events might look like this:

> History of Chocolate
>
> | 1500 B.C. | Olmec Indians grew cocoa beans as crop. Unsweetened drink. |
> | 1544 | Mixed cocoa drink intro → Spain/Portugal |
> | 16th c. | Spanish: + sugar → sweet cocoa drink |
> | 1674 | 1st solid chocolate |

CUES TO RECOGNIZE A PROCESS OR SEQUENCE OF EVENTS

1. Time expressions that signal a sequence of events or steps in a process:

   First (second, third), . . .
   Next (Then, Subsequently, Later, After that), . . .
   Prior to (Previously, Before that), . . .
   By the end of this year . . .
   It will take (another several weeks) . . .
   Over the next (two years) . . .
   In 1965 (In the first century), . . .
   Originally . . . (but) now . . .

2. Phrases or sentences that signal a sequence of events or steps in a process:

   The first (second, next) step is . . .
   In order to arrive at this point, we had to . . .
   It starts out with . . . and then . . .
   We can trace the development . . .

   Let's look at {
   how this came about
   where this comes from
   how to X
   (the steps involved in) this process
   }

3. Rhetorical questions that signal a description of a process or sequence of events:

Where did this idea come from?
How can we do this?
How did this come about?

Exercise 2

 You will hear three lecture excerpts that include descriptions of processes or sequences of events. First, read the information about each excerpt. Then, while listening to the excerpt, take notes in the spaces provided.

Example
Excerpt from an anthropology lecture

Heading | Neanderthal finds
Sequence | Found in Neander Valley, Germany
         | Farmer found it: 1856: 1ˢᵗ find
         | Defined as EARLY HUMAN
         | Thought it was deformed/odd human
         |
         | Not talked about until ~ 1865
         | Why? publish Darwin's "Origin of Species"

1. Excerpt from a lecture on business and technology (cell phone innovations)

Heading | Cell phone use:
        | Current world pop: 6.3 billion
Sequence | Cellular connectivity (by end of yr.):

2. Excerpt from a lecture on sleep biology

Stages of sleep: not a continuous period of sleep but 90 min. cycles all night

   — 10 min: start w/ very light sleep

   — (over next 45 min.) _____

   — (after about 1 hr.) _____

   — _____

3. Excerpt from a lecture on library research (The speaker has already talked about the first three steps, as noted below. Listen and note the next three steps.)

First 8 Steps for Library Research

   1. survey topic (look for broadest discussion) and clarify unfamiliar terms

   2. break topic into simple subtopics

   3. look for types of info. needed to research subject

   4.

   5.

   6.

C Classifying Subtopics

With classifying subtopics, the lecturer's goal is to make a topic more manageable by creating classifications to organize the information from the larger topic.

A **classification** provides headings so that information can be grouped together based on similar characteristics. For example, a geologist may present a lecture on rocks by talking about the three different kinds of rocks: igneous, sedimentary, and metamorphic. If the lecture compared the types while describing them, it would be a combination of a classification organizational plan and a comparison/contrast organizational plan.

Notes from a lecture presenting a classification might look like this:

Mammals: Animals w/ body hair, warm-blooded, nourish young with milk fr. ♀

3 types:

   Marsupials: young- born very immature.

     Most ♀ have pouch

       e.g. kangaroo, opossums

   Monotremes: primitive, lay eggs

     e.g. platypus

   Placental mammals: advanced; unborn young nourished w/ placenta.

     e.g. humans, elephants

Alternatively, these notes might be organized in columns:

Mammals: animals w/ body hair, warm-blooded, nourish young w/ milk fr. ♀

Marsupials	Monotremes	Placental Mammals
young-born very immature	primitive	advanced
most ♀ have pouch	lay eggs	unborn young nourished w/ placenta
e.g. kangaroo, opossum	e.g. platypus	e.g. humans, elephants

CUES TO RECOGNIZE CLASSIFICATIONS

1. Phrases that indicate categories:

X can be { *divided / subdivided / broken down / classified* } *into two (three, four)* { *groups / schools of thought / divisions / categories / classifications* }

There are two (three, four) { *types of / schools of thought about / divisions of / classifications of* } *X*

2. Rhetorical questions that signal classifications:

What types of X are there?
How can X be classified/categorized?

Exercise 3

You will hear three lecture excerpts that include classifications. First, read the information about each excerpt. Then, while listening to the excerpt, take notes in the spaces provided.

Example
Excerpt from a lecture on family systems

Heading
Classifications

> Types of households
> — patrilocal   — couple lives w/ husband's father
> — virilocal   — couple lives w/ husband's family — not father
> — matrilocal   —   "   "   wife's mother
> — uxorilocal   —   "   "   wife's family — not mother

1. Excerpt from a lecture on human development in the womb

   VOCABULARY

   womb: the place in the mother's body where the fetus develops
   conception: the forming of an embryo; the beginning of pregnancy

Heading

Classifications

3 periods of development in womb		
1.	2.	3.

2. Excerpt from a lecture on eight steps to topic analysis for library research

Heading

Classifications

> 3rd step — Look for types of info. needed to research subject
> —
> —

3. Excerpt from a lecture on marriage systems

   VOCABULARY

   spouse: a husband or wife

Heading

Classifications

Subclassifications

> Two kinds of polygamy (plural spouses)
> &

Archaeological Dating Methods   (Anthropology)

Vocabulary

Related to Archaeology

Check (✔) the words you know. Underline the words you want to learn. Then check their meaning with your instructor or in a dictionary.

excavation
dig

site

remains
remnants
ruins

excavate

inhabit/inhabitant
reside/resident
dwell/dweller

shelter
residence
dwelling

tribe
clan

legend
myth

archaeologist

ACTIVITY **1** **PRE-LECTURE READING AND DISCUSSION**

Read this excerpt from a scientific magazine describing life more than 3,000 years ago.

The description is not from a particular site; rather, it is made up of details discovered at several archaeological digs. There are no written records of these events, no pictures or legends passed down through the years.

The site was first inhabited in 1250 B.C. by a small tribe of forty or fifty men, women, and children. The women wore bright beaded jewelry, and many of the men had their front teeth sanded down,[1] perhaps as a symbol of bravery.

They came from somewhere farther north, searching for food and shelter. On their arrival, they felled several dozen trees near the creek, choosing only the hardest woods to carve into tent poles. There was an accident and one young brave died of ax[2] wounds.[3]

That spring over 3,000 years ago, the men went out on a hunt, bringing down at least seventy young bison[4]—enough to keep the tribe well fed and clothed. The carcasses[5] were hauled to a cave in the nearby mountainside for butchering. Most of the meat was later roasted over open fire pits in the valley below, while the tougher parts were stone-boiled for soup. For this kind of cooking, stones were heated in a fire until red-hot. Then the stones were placed in a pot of water to make the water boil.

The bones of the bison were kept in the cave. Some were whittled[6] into tools, but only two of the best tribal craftsmen were allowed to handle this job. The unusable bones were dumped into a garbage heap toward the back of the cave.

While the men hunted, the women gathered nuts and berries. Hackberries were the favorite. That first year was a prosperous[7] one. Over twenty-three inches of rain fell. The area provided sustenance[8] for over a hundred species of animals and dozens of varieties of plants. The tribe could keep a few wild dogs as pets.

A wandering[9] tradesman came to visit that year and brought seeds for a new kind of edible plant—seeds that the women used to start a crop. The visitor also brought trinkets[10]: turquoise beads and strange bits of a sharp-edged material called obsidian, which had been found near a faraway volcano. Together with bits of shell and animal teeth, these were brought to the women's work tent to make more necklaces.

In the year 1245 B.C., a great drought[11] hit the area, followed by a hard winter. Crops shriveled.[12] The creek dried out. Many of the tribespeople, including an eight-month-old baby and a seventy-year-old tribal elder, died from hunger or cold. The tribe resorted to cannibalism, eating the remains of their dead to keep alive.

The area began to change. The forests and fields were replaced by a parched[13] and dusty landscape.

---

[1] **sand (down):** to smooth or reduce something, using sand or rough paper
[2] **ax:** a cutting tool with a sharp metal head and a wooden handle
[3] **wound:** an injury
[4] **bison:** a buffalo-like animal
[5] **carcass:** the body of a dead animal
[6] **whittle:** to cut off small pieces (of wood, bone) with a knife

[7] **prosperous:** successful
[8] **sustenance:** anything that gives support or health or strength
[9] **wander:** to move from place to place
[10] **trinket:** a piece of jewelry or a small, pretty object, often of little value
[11] **drought:** a long period without rain
[12] **shrivel:** to become drier and smaller
[13] **parched:** very dry

While you were reading, were you surprised at how much archaeologists were able to learn about life so long ago? Do you know how they were able to reach these conclusions?

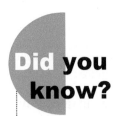

Did you know?

Evidence suggests that the first human beings lived in caves along the southern coast of Africa.

Work in small groups to suggest what evidence might have led the archaeologists to each of these conclusions. Use your imagination and your knowledge. The first one has been done as an example. When you are finished, discuss your ideas as a class. Which seem like the best answers?

Conclusion	Possible Evidence
1. The site was inhabited by forty to fifty men, women, and children.	*They found skeletons.*
2. The women wore bright beaded jewelry.	
3. The men had their front teeth sanded down, perhaps as a symbol of bravery.	
4. They came from somewhere farther north, searching for food and shelter.	
5. On their arrival, they cut down several dozen trees near the creek, choosing only the hardest woods to carve into tent poles.	
6. There was an accident and one young brave died of ax wounds.	
7. That spring, the men went out on a hunt, bringing down at least seventy young bison.	
8. The carcasses were hauled to a cave in the nearby mountainside for butchering.	
9. Most of the meat was roasted over open fire pits in the valley below while the tougher parts were stone-boiled for soup.	
10. Only two of the best tribal craftsmen were allowed to handle the job of whittling bones into tools.	
11. That first year over twenty-three inches of rain fell.	
12. A wandering tradesman came to visit that year and brought seeds for a new kind of edible plant—seeds that the women used to start a crop.	
13. In the year 1245 B.C., a great drought hit the area, followed by a hard winter.	
14. The tribe was forced to move on in search of better hunting grounds.	

ACTIVITY ② PREPARING FOR THE LECTURE

The title of the lecture is "Archaeological Dating Methods." What do you expect the lecturer to say about this? Brainstorm ideas with your classmates.

🎧 **Listen to the beginning of the lecture. Then answer the following question:**

True or false?

_____ The lecture is going to give an overview of all the methods archaeologists use to date material.

ACTIVITY ③ LISTENING FOR THE LARGER PICTURE

🎧 **Read the following statements before the lecture begins. Then, listen to the lecture once without taking notes. After listening, fill in the blanks.**

The lecturer talks about two different archaeological dating methods:

_____ and _____.

In particular, the lecturer talks about the latter method's drawbacks and recent

_____.

ACTIVITY ④ ORGANIZATION

Read this summary of the lecture organization.

> The overall organizational plan of this lecture is **exemplification**. The topic is archaeological dating methods, and two examples of these dating methods are discussed in detail. In addition, the lecture includes an explanation of a **process**—the process of C-14 dating.

Do you remember anything about the two archaeological dating methods that were discussed? Do you remember anything about the process of C-14 dating? Discuss with a partner.

Archaeologists at work on a site in New Mexico.

The following words and expressions were used in the lecture that you just heard. You may remember the contexts in which you heard them.

Match the word with the meaning.

_____ 1. *Climatic* change is occurring worldwide.

_____ 2. Don't sit on that chair. It's *unstable**, and you might fall.

_____ 3. If you want to be more certain of the results of your experiment, don't forget to *cross-check* your results.

_____ 4. We thought that spring had arrived, but the recent *cold spell* reminded us that it was still a few months away.

_____ 5. It's a desirable location for farming because there is always an *abundant* supply of water.

_____ 6. The poll looked at a *cross-section* of the population.

_____ 7. I found an old letter, but it *disintegrated* in my hands when I picked it up to read it.

_____ 8. The sound of the train *diminished** as it got farther away.

_____ 9. The workers *tallied* the votes and declared her the winner.

_____ 10. The sun *emits* heat.

_____ 11. Nothing is perfect. Everything has *drawbacks*.

_____ 12. The recent *drought* caused people to leave their land in search of food and water.

a. to release; to send out

b. to count

c. a part or sample that is typical of a larger group or thing

d. a long period of dry weather when there is insufficient water

e. limitations; disadvantages or difficulties

f. to break into very small pieces

g. to get smaller (in strength or effect)

h. relating to weather patterns

i. a long period of cold weather

j. in large quantities

k. easily moved, upset, or changed; not firm

l. to find out the correctness of something by using a different method, standard, or information from other places

Listen to the lecture a second time. Take notes using the following format. The comments in the left margin serve to remind you of the organization of the lecture.

Introduction	*Archaeological Dating Methods*
Example 1: Dendrochronology	*Dendrochronology*
Details	
Example 2: C-14 dating	*Carbon-14 dating method*
Process	

Drawbacks	Drawbacks of C-14 method
Advances	Recent advances in C-14 dating: Accelerated Mass Spectrometry (AMS)
Limitations	C-14 dating is limited to _____ years
Conclusions	

ACTIVITY 7 **REPLAY QUESTION**

🎧 **Listen to a section of the lecture. Then answer the question.**

Why did the lecturer bring up the shroud in Italy?

_____ **a.** He wanted to give an example of successful radiocarbon dating.

_____ **b.** He wanted to give an example showing why people might oppose radiocarbon dating of some objects.

_____ **c.** He wanted to give an example of destruction caused by radiocarbon dating.

_____ **d.** It was a digression from the main part of the lecture and he wanted to entertain students.

LISTENING AND NOTE-TAKING STRATEGIES

1. Review your notes as soon as possible after listening. Perhaps there was information that you heard but did not have time to note. Add information that you remember.

2. Work with a partner to ask for information that you missed or are unsure about.

3. Consider rewriting your notes soon after listening. You can make the relationship between ideas more clear and make important ideas stand out by indenting or using headings, for example.

Listen to the first part of a conversation in a professor's office and answer the first question.

1. The student is considering a major in anthropology, but she wants to talk to the professor about two concerns. What are they?

   a. What _____?

   b. What _____?

Listen to more of the conversation and answer the rest of the questions.

2. The professor does not immediately answer the student's questions. Instead, in order to help the student, the professor asks his own questions. What are they?

   a. _____

   b. _____

3. What advice does the professor give the student about finding her focus in anthropology?

   _____

   _____

   _____

4. What is the professor's advice about choosing a major?

   _____ a. Consider the job prospects before choosing a major.

   _____ b. Follow your heart when choosing a major.

   _____ c. Listen to your parents when choosing a major.

   _____ d. Talk to an advisor about choosing a major.

5. The conversation is not over. Write three additional questions that the student might ask the professor about this topic.

   _____

   _____

   _____

ACTIVITY 9 POST-LECTURE READING AND DISCUSSION

Would you be interested in working with researchers who are investigating the prehistoric past? Earthwatch Institute International is an international nonprofit organization that supports scientific field research through programs that put volunteers and scientists together at a research site. Though projects often take years, volunteers join the team for one to three weeks.

Read through the following project descriptions to answer these questions about each one:

- What are the researchers trying to find out?
- What will volunteers be doing?
- What are the working and living conditions? (Consider site, climate, recreation opportunities.)

After reading the descriptions, decide which program would best fit your interests and preferences. In small groups, explain your choice and at least three of your reasons.

Project 1:

Dinosaur Footprints

Dinosaur footprint

Yorkshire, England. Just as a good tracker today can tell you what animal made a track,[1] its age, sex, size, speed of travel, and something about its behavior ("It's headed north toward the river"), a good detective can read similar information from the footprints of extinct[2] creatures, such as dinosaurs. If you're lacking[3] physical remains—as is often true of the middle Jurassic dinosaurs of 165 million years ago, when many groups of dinosaurs were developing— then the tracks they left become even more critical. One track Dr. Martin Whyte and Dr. Mike Romano (of the University of Sheffield, England) have found, for instance, was from a sauropod[4] dinosaur, which they estimated to be about six feet at the hip joint and up to thirty-five feet long. He was plodding[5] along at half a mile an hour. Was he eating? Did he have companions? Was he full-grown? Was he a she?

Paleontologists[6] have long known that the spectacular seacoast of Yorkshire harbored lots of dinosaur tracks, but you have the chance to be among the first to locate, systematically study, and help preserve them. You'll search along the shore and valleys for footprints. The data that teams collect will help determine the number and proportions of species over time that made Yorkshire home, and the size, behavior, and speed of the footprint-makers. Your findings will help piece together what kinds of dinosaurs once roamed[7] Yorkshire, how they lived and evolved,[8] and what their world was like.

RESEARCH AREA

The Heritage Coastline is a national park encompassing cliffs and sandy bays. Nearby towns are littered with Roman, Viking, and medieval ruins.[9] Expect typically British weather: changeable from blue skies to fog to rain, and daytime temperatures around 60° F (15° C).

VOLUNTEER TASKS

Working in small crews, volunteers will search the coastline and valleys for dinosaur footprints. Teams will map, photograph, and trace prints; teams will also help make casts of selected tracks and record geological features. Skills in photography, drawing, mapping, and geological survey will come in handy. Be prepared to climb steep valley sides.

---

[1] *track:* signs of animal movement such as footprints
[2] *extinct:* describing a plant or animal which no longer exists
[3] *lack:* to not have
[4] *sauropod:* a type of dinosaur
[5] *plod (along):* to move very slowly
[6] *paleontologist:* a scientist who studies ancient life
[7] *roam:* to move aimlessly from place to place
[8] *evolve:* to develop over time
[9] *medieval ruins:* broken parts of old buildings from medieval times (Middle Ages: 476–1450 A.D.)

Search for Neanderthals

Prehistoric tools

Sima de las Palomas and Cueva Negra, Murcia, Spain. Two years ago, Dr. Michael Walker (of Murcia University, Spain) began excavating Cueva Negra ("Black Cave") in the mountains of southeastern Spain. His efforts have been rewarded with discoveries of teeth from Neanderthal humans, remnants of extinct animals, and the stone tools used to butcher those animals.

The second site, named Cabezo Gordo ("Big Hill"), was discovered accidentally in 1991 when a young explorer, investigating an old mine,[1] inadvertently[2] dislodged[3] a bone with human teeth attached. The remains were indeed those of Neanderthal Man. Subsequent[4] excavations of this site have yielded[5] the remains of twenty Neanderthals, together with their tools and the bones of extinct animals, including lions and panthers, that had also inhabited this site.

Paleoanthropologists want to learn more about Neanderthals, who disappeared from the archaeological record about 35,000 years ago. Were the Neanderthals the true ancestors of modern humans in Europe? Was Europe populated by travelers from the Near East or Africa after the Neanderthals died out? Perhaps some of the information we discover in Murcia will help answer those questions.

RESEARCH AREA

Both research sites are located in the province of Murcia in southeastern Spain. Murcia is extremely dry during the summer months with a very warm coastal region (85° F to 105° F; 30° C to 40° C). Murcia, an important Muslim kingdom until the thirteenth century, was once known for its silk industry. Mulberry orchards have since been replaced by peaches, tomatoes, lemons, oranges, almonds, and olives.

VOLUNTEER TASKS

Earthwatch team members will be assigned to task groups and will have the opportunity to work on all aspects of the project. Morning assignments will involve excavation and removing excavated material for sieving.[6] Afternoon assignments will include washing and drying excavated materials from the morning's work and preliminary classification of the dry materials from the previous day.

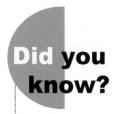

Did you know?

The oldest pottery in the world is Jomon pottery of Japan, which is about 16,000 years old.

---

[1] *mine:* an underground place from which minerals are removed
[2] *inadvertently:* unintentionally, accidentally
[3] *dislodge:* to move out of a fixed position
[4] *subsequent:* following
[5] *yield:* to produce
[6] *sieving:* using a sieve (a round wire tool for separating small objects from large objects)

Use your notes to answer the following questions.

1. Which statement is *not* true?

    ____ **a.** In order to do a dendrochronological analysis, scientists must count all the tree rings.

    ____ **b.** By doing a dendrochronological analysis, scientists can tell when a drought or a cold spell occurred.

    ____ **c.** Dendrochronological analyses are limited to only about a few thousand years.

    ____ **d.** The carbon-14 dating method is based on the idea that all living organisms contain C-14, a radioactive isotope.

2. Which statement is true?

    ____ **a.** The carbon-14 dating method is based on the idea that an organism's carbon-14 level changes while it is alive.

    ____ **b.** One drawback of the C-14 dating method is that the radioactivity is dangerous to the researcher.

    ____ **c.** Accelerator Mass Spectrometry measures the C-14 atoms, not the radioactive emissions.

    ____ **d.** Carbon-14 dating does not work well with objects older than 16,000 years.

3. True or false?

    ____ Most of the time, scientists use at least two dating methods in order to ensure accuracy.

4. A pale tree ring indicates

    ____ **a.** winter   ____ **c.** a drought   ____ **e.** abundant water and sunlight

    ____ **b.** spring   ____ **d.** a cold spell

5. A thick tree ring indicates

    ____ **a.** winter   ____ **c.** a drought   ____ **e.** abundant water and sunlight

    ____ **b.** spring   ____ **d.** a cold spell

6. What is the half-life of C-14? _____

7. How is Accelerated Mass Spectrometer dating an improvement over older C-14 dating methods?

    _____

    _____

8. Describe how an archaeologist would conduct a dendrochronological analysis.

    _____

    _____

1. In small groups, compare your answers to the preceding questions. If you have different answers, check your notes and discuss your reasons for making your choices.

2. Compare your rewritten notes to the sample rewritten notes in Appendix D. Notice the organization. Is yours similar or different? Are your notes equally effective in making important ideas stand out?

ACTIVITY **12** **ACADEMIC WORD LIST VOCABULARY**

Match the word and its meaning. Write the correct letter in the space provided. An example is given of the word in context.

Group 1
  a. to believe something is true without knowing for sure
  b. to change or differ
  c. to lessen in force, number, or quality
  d. to center one's attention; to concentrate
  e. to experience; to go through a difficult process

_____ 1. *diminish*   I'm worried about our diminishing supply of water. See if you can get more.

_____ 2. *focus*   Stop daydreaming; let's focus on the task at hand.

_____ 3. *assume*   We assumed she was American because she spoke English without an accent.

_____ 4. *undergo*   The student had to undergo multiple blood tests before they could diagnose the problem.

_____ 5. *vary*   He varied his route to work each day so he wouldn't get bored.

Group 2
  a. a technique; a way of doing something
  b. practical applications of science and engineering theory
  c. something on a list; a thing or object
  d. a study that examines the nature of something

_____ 6. *method*   She taught us a method for remembering words.

_____ 7. *analysis*   Analysis of the blood sample indicated a serious iron deficiency.

_____ 8. *technology*   Stone-age cultures had limited technology, but they were able to use some tools and the wheel.

_____ 9. *item*   How many items did you get wrong on the test?

Group 3
- **a.** exact; precise
- **b.** main; most important
- **c.** almost alike
- **d.** enough; adequate
- **e.** not steady; not firm

____ **10.** *major*   I agree with your major points, but I disagree with some of the details.

____ **11.** *sufficient*   Because there wasn't sufficient water that year, many crops died.

____ **12.** *unstable*   Be careful on that ladder; it's a little unstable.

____ **13.** *accurate*   Is this thermometer accurate? It doesn't feel that hot here.

____ **14.** *similar*   Their cultures are similar because their ancestors had originally come from the same area.

ACTIVITY **13** **USING VOCABULARY**

Listen to each item. Then, paraphrase what you hear by filling in the blanks with words from the vocabulary list. (You may change the verb forms and tenses.)

legends	*deteriorate*	*drought*	*site*
drawback	*diminish*	*inhabitants*	*emit*
cold spell	*excavate*	*abundant*	*assume*

1. According to _____, a very powerful tribe of people lived at this _____. Archaeologists _____ the area in order to find out the truth.

2. An analysis of a cross-section of the tree indicates a _____ during the year 2000 B.C. that _____ the food supply.

3. The primary _____ of the older C-14 dating method is that it requires a fairly large sample.

4. In 1450, there was a period of _____ rainfall, and this caused the _____ to move to higher ground.

5. In 1550, there was a _____ and scientists _____ this is the reason the people moved once again.

> **VOCABULARY STRATEGY**
>
> When you learn new words, learn their different forms.

ADJECTIVES	NOUNS	ADVERBS	VERBS
abundant	abundance	abundantly	
unstable	instability		destabilize
	emission		emit
	disintegration		disintegrate
residential	resident; residence		reside
mythical	myth	mythically	
tribal	tribe	tribally	

Fill in the blank with the correct form of the word. Letters of the words are given as clues.

1. The *resid*_____ of the house had to leave because the earthquake had made the structure _____*stab*_____.

2. According to *trib*_____ myths, the fruit trees produced *abund*_____ even during the drought. How could that be?

3. The animal *em*_____ an odor that caused other animals to flee.

4. New laws have been passed to control *em*_____ from cars and factories.

5. The paper *dis*_____ and turned to dust in her hands.

6. The goddess of corn is a *m*_____ being, but the people believe she exists.

7. The failure of farms and businesses led to _____ *stab*_____ in the economy.

8. This is a *resid*_____ area, so please be quiet at night.

9. Don't believe that story. It's only a *m*_____.

Complete the following assignment.

Write a letter to the director of Earthwatch Institute International, expressing your interest in volunteering for one of the projects on pages 113–114. A formal letter of interest might look like this:

Jan Seymour
13 Harvard Way
New York, NY 10011

March 4, 2010

Earthwatch Institute International
3 Clock Tower Place, Suite 100
Box 75
Maynard, MA 01754

To Whom It May Concern,

Recently, I had a chance to examine your Web site and read about your volunteer opportunities.

(In your letter, explain why the project interests you and what skills you have that might be useful for the project. Add questions that you might have about the project, the research area, the living conditions, and the volunteer activities.)

I look forward to hearing from you.

Sincerely,

Jan Seymour

Pheromones   (Biology)

Vocabulary

Related to Animal Communication and Pheromones

Check (✓) the words you know. Underline the words you want to learn. Then check their meaning with your instructor or in a dictionary.

animal kingdom
nocturnal animal
aquatic animal
terrestrial animal

species

mammal
reptile
insect
amphibian
crustacean
primate
rodent

predator
prey

migrate

mate

hive
den
nest
lair

Is that a new perfume you're wearing?

ACTIVITY **1** **PRE-LECTURE DISCUSSION**

Discuss the following questions.

Do you know how ants communicate the location of food sources to other ants? How do bees determine the location of their particular bee colony? How do snails mate and communicate the desire to mate to other snails? Do you know about any other types of animal communication systems? If so, describe them.

ACTIVITY **2** **PREPARING FOR THE LECTURE**

The title of the lecture is "Pheromones." Find a definition of *pheromone* in the dictionary. Based on this definition and the previous discussion questions, what do you expect the lecturer to talk about? Brainstorm ideas with your classmates.

 At the beginning of the lecture, the speaker gives an extended definition of the term *pheromone*. Listen and take notes.

Pheromone:

How does the lecturer's definition compare to your dictionary definition?

ACTIVITY **3** **LISTENING FOR THE LARGER PICTURE**

Read the following questions before the lecture begins. Then, listen to the lecture once without taking notes. While listening, answer the questions.

1. The lecturer's goal is to tell the audience about pheromones. How does the lecturer do this? Check (✓) as many as are correct.

   _____ a. Defines the term *pheromone*

   _____ b. Shows the similarities and differences between pheromones and other forms of animal communication

   _____ c. Classifies the types of pheromones

   _____ d. Gives examples of different kinds of pheromones

   _____ e. Describes the chemical makeup of pheromones

2. Which of the following are characteristics of pheromones? Check (✓) as many as are correct.

   _____ a. Pheromones may be detected by the sense of smell or taste.

   _____ b. Pheromones may be detected by any species nearby.

   _____ c. Pheromones are very sensitive and require only small amounts to get a response.

   _____ d. Pheromones may be detected by the sense of touch.

   _____ e. Pheromones must be produced in great quantities in order to be effective.

   _____ f. Each particular species is responsive only to its own species' pheromones.

   _____ g. The pheromones of one species have no effect on members of other species.

3. There are two types of pheromones: primer pheromones and releaser pheromones. How do they differ? _____

   _____

4. How many types of releaser pheromones does the speaker mention? _____

Read this summary of the lecture organization.

> The lecture primarily demonstrates three organizational plans: **defining a term**, **classifying**, and **exemplifying**. The lecturer defines *pheromone* by giving a simple definition and then expanding it by adding characteristics of pheromones. The lecturer then classifies pheromones into two types, *primer* and *releaser pheromones*, and further classifies releaser pheromones into four types, giving additional definitions and examples for each one.

Do you remember anything about the different types of releaser pheromones and the examples that were discussed? Discuss with a partner.

ACTIVITY **5** **DEFINING VOCABULARY**

The following words and expressions were used in the lecture that you just heard. You may remember the contexts in which you heard them.

You will hear an additional example of each word or expression in a new context. After listening, check (✓) the letter of the definition that most closely matches what you think the word or expression means.

1. *emit*

 _____ **a.** to smell something

 _____ **b.** to send out

 _____ **c.** to take responsibility for

2. *evoke a response**

 _____ **a.** to respond (*to* someone else)

 _____ **b.** to bring out a response (*from* someone else)

 _____ **c.** to refuse to respond

3. *physiological*

 _____ **a.** related to biological processes

 _____ **b.** related to the mind

 _____ **c.** related to the science of physics

4. *mutually* exclusive**

 _____ **a.** occurring together

 _____ **b.** not occurring together

 _____ **c.** exchanging basic parts

5. *disperse*

____ a. to separate and move into various directions

____ b. to commit a crime; to perform an unlawful act

____ c. to give an order; to command

6. *flee*

____ a. to burn; to burst into flames

____ b. to live; to reside

____ c. to run away; to escape

7. *stimulant*

____ a. a substance that helps one sleep

____ b. a substance that temporarily increases physiological activity

____ c. a substance that one drinks

8. *arouse*

____ a. to scare away

____ b. to excite

____ c. to point out the direction

9. *terrestrial*

____ a. related to land

____ b. related to water

____ c. related to air

10. *navigational guide*

____ a. something that produces light

____ b. something that contains water

____ c. something that leads one on a particular path

11. *exhaust*

____ a. to increase the use of

____ b. to use completely

____ c. to continue the use of

12. *insecticide*

____ a. a substance used to protect insects

____ b. a substance used to kill insects

____ c. a substance used to encourage insects to reproduce

Listen to the lecture a second time. Take notes using the following format. The comments in the left margin serve to remind you of the organization of the lecture.

Definition	Pheromones—
Details about definition	
Classifications	Types of pheromones:
Definitions and examples	primer pheromone
	e.g.
	releaser pheromone
	alarm pheromone
	e.g.
	aggregation pheromone
	e.g.
	sex pheromone
	e.g.
	terrestrial trail pheromone
	e.g.
Conclusions	

ACTIVITY **7** **REPLAY QUESTION**

Listen to a section of the lecture. Fill in the blanks with the words that the lecturer used to show **contrasting** ideas.

Now the primer pheromones cause physiological changes in the organism and affect its development and later behavior . . . Okay now the releaser pheromones _____ *produce rapid and reversible responses and immediate changes . . . so* _____ *the primer pheromones are long-range . . . not reversible . . . the releaser pheromones are rapid . . . immediate . . . and reversible.*

LISTENING AND NOTE-TAKING STRATEGIES

1. Review your notes as soon as possible after listening. Perhaps there was information that you heard but did not have time to note. Add information that you remember.

2. Work with a partner to ask for information that you missed or are unsure about.

3. Consider rewriting your notes soon after listening. You can make the relationship between ideas clearer and make important ideas stand out by indenting or using headings, for example.

ACTIVITY **8** **"OTHER VOICES" FOLLOW-UP**

A student stops in to see a professor. Listen to the conversation in the office. Then answer the questions.

1. What was the student's *stated* reason for coming to the professor's office?

____ a. He wanted to talk about his career and study plans.

____ b. He wanted to share an article he found online.

____ c. He did not understand something in class and wanted more information.

____ d. He was worried about how he was doing in the class.

2. The student initially stated one reason for coming to the professor's office, but it is possible to *infer* other reasons. (When you make an inference, you make a logical or reasonable guess based on the information you have.) Which of the following are inferences that you can make about the student's visit? Check (✓) two.

____ a. The student is considering dropping the class.

____ b. The student is concerned about a paper that is due.

____ c. The student is worried about failing the class.

____ d. The student wants to make a good impression on the professor.

Discuss the following in small groups.

1. The lecturer discusses pheromones and their function in the animal kingdom. However, the lecturer does not mention humans. Do you think humans are influenced by pheromones? If so, how?

2. Read the article below. Then discuss your answers to the questions that follow.

Researchers Sniff[1] Out[2] Pheromones

Gwenda Blair, *Los Angeles Times*

If the idea of using smell to find a mate[3] sounds like a stretch,[4] consider a further stretch: pheromones, long-sought[5] odorless but gender-specific chemical signals exchanged by most mammals but until recently believed to be extinct in humans.

A few years ago, Dr. Louis Monti-Bloch, a physiologist at the University of Utah, teamed up with Dr. David Berliner, a former anatomist, and tested what they believed were human pheromones on volunteers. They reported that these elicited[6] an electrical response near the volunteers' nostrils. Further, Berliner claimed, responses to pheromones were gender-specific. Unlike odors, which almost always affect women more than men, pheromones evoked an equally strong reaction in men and women.

Berliner promptly patented[7] these substances and founded a company called Erox to manufacture them. Most of the scientific establishment remains skeptical,[8] however. For one thing, says Michael Meredith, a biologist at Florida State University, Berliner and Monti-Bloch's work has not been replicated.[9] And Berliner's haste[10] to make a profit from his research seems, well, unseemly[11] to his peers.

Yet supporting evidence is slowly accumulating.[12] For example, Martha McClintock, a biopsychologist at the University of Chicago, confirmed that a group of women living together in a college dormitory tend to synchronize[13] menstrual cycles,[14] which many consider a pheromonal effect. Researchers from the University of Bern, Switzerland, found that when women were asked to choose among T-shirts worn by men who were strangers, they mysteriously selected those of men whose immune systems,[15] according to DNA analyses, were most unlike their own—possible evidence of a built-in smell-based preference for mates who could help produce offspring[16] with wide immunological coverage, researchers speculated.[17]

The upshot:[18] Don't spend any money on a pheromonal spritz,[19] but if you're attracted to a stranger's T-shirt, don't assume it's the logo[20] you like!

---

[1] *sniff:* to smell or breathe in air in a way that others can hear
[2] *sniff out:* to discover evidence
[3] *mate:* a spouse; husband or wife
[4] *stretch:* something hard to believe
[5] *sought:* (*past tense of seek*): searched; looked for
[6] *elicit:* to get or bring out (a response)
[7] *patent:* to gain legal rights to make, use, and sell an invention for a period of time
[8] *skeptical:* doubtful

[9] *replicate:* to copy
[10] *haste:* speed; quickness
[11] *unseemly:* inappropriate
[12] *accumulate:* to gather together
[13] *synchronize:* to match (in time)
[14] *menstrual cycle:* women's monthly bleeding
[15] *immune system:* the system that protects people from disease
[16] *offspring:* children
[17] *speculate:* to guess about
[18] *upshot:* conclusion
[19] *spritz:* (*informal*): a spray
[20] *logo:* a design symbol (of a product)

a. How many research studies are discussed in this article? What did each research study find?

b. Why are Berliner's peers skeptical of his work?

c. Does this article support the idea that pheromones are extinct in humans?

d. In some magazines, you might see advertisements that offer pheromone-based lotions that are supposed to attract members of the opposite sex. Based on the information in the article, would you believe these claims? Why or why not?

ACTIVITY 10 **USING YOUR NOTES**

Did you know?

Bee stings, an alarm pheromone, not only wound an enemy but also alert other bees to danger and, in some cases, cause swarming.

Use your notes to answer the following questions on a separate piece of paper.

1. Define the term *pheromone* as used in the lecture.

2. True or false?

_____ a. Pheromones are used by a variety of species ranging from one-celled animals to higher primates (i.e., an order including monkeys, apes, and humans).

_____ b. An example of a primer pheromone is when an animal releases a pheromone that calls other animals to attack.

_____ c. An example of a primer pheromone is when a female snail releases a pheromone that causes a sexually undifferentiated snail to develop into a male.

_____ d. Primer pheromones cause psychological changes.

_____ e. Bees find their way back to their hives because of terrestrial trail pheromones.

_____ f. Pheromones can be used to control animal behavior for crop protection.

_____ g. Pheromones can harm people who eat crops grown near to where the pheromones were used.

_____ h. The four types of releaser pheromones are mutually exclusive.

3. Pheromones are said to be "highly sensitive" and "highly specific." Explain these concepts.

4. Contrast the terms *primer pheromone* and *releaser pheromone*.

5. In a paragraph, discuss the different types of releaser pheromones in terms of their functions. Give an example of how each pheromone type can be observed in the animal kingdom.

1. In small groups, compare your answers to the preceding questions. If you have different answers, check your notes and discuss your reasons for making your choices.

2. Compare your rewritten notes to the sample rewritten notes in Appendix D. Notice the organization. Is yours similar or different? Are your notes equally effective in making important ideas stand out?

ACTIVITY **12** ACADEMIC WORD LIST VOCABULARY

Match the word and its meaning. Write the correct letter in the space provided. An example is given of the word in context.

Group 1
a. to let out; to issue
b. to continue; to keep something going
c. to find; to notice; to observe
d. to change to the opposite or backwards
e. to make something possible

____ 1. *detect*   He couldn't detect the source of the gas odor.

____ 2. *maintain*   How do you maintain contact with your old classmates?

____ 3. *reverse*   She reversed directions when she realized that she was lost.

____ 4. *enable*   Her salary raise enabled her to buy a better car.

____ 5. *release*   The newspapers were waiting for the zoo to release information about the baby panda.

Group 2
a. mainly
b. working both ways; balanced in both directions
c. alone; singly
d. sufficiently; enough
e. easy to understand or see

____ 6. *adequately*   The animals were adequately cared for, but it wasn't the best of zoos.

____ 7. *primarily*   In much of the animal kingdom, childcare is primarily a maternal responsibility.

____ 8. *mutually*   The arrangement was mutually satisfactory to both the employer and employee.

____ 9. *solely*   She was solely responsible for the care of the tiger.

____ 10. *obviously*   That gorilla is obviously the leader of the group; you can see that within a few minutes.

Group 3
a. use or purpose
b. atmosphere or surroundings
c. the limits or extremes between which something is possible
d. a custom or belief passed from one generation to another
e. a group or type of something

_____ 11. *function*   She explained the function of the tool and then demonstrated it.

_____ 12. *range*   His professional interests cover a range of subjects from astronomy to zoology.

_____ 13. *category*   We have different categories of jobs, mainly divided between those that are office-based and those that are road-based.

_____ 14. *environment*   Changes in the environment certainly affect the availability of food for local animals.

_____ 15. *tradition*   Does your family have any traditions for celebrating holidays or birthdays?

ACTIVITY 13 **USING VOCABULARY**

You will hear vocabulary from this lecture in different contexts. Listen before reading each paragraph. After listening, fill in the blanks with words from the vocabulary list to paraphrase the information that you heard. (You may change the verb forms and tenses.)

1. *stimulants   insecticides   navigational guides   physiological changes*

Workers at the chemical company complained of stomach pains. Examinations of the chemicals that they were using did, in fact, demonstrate that they acted as _____, causing _____ in subjects.

2. *flee   emit   disperse   evoke a response   exhaust*

The refugees were forced to_____ their homeland. Because it was dangerous to leave in groups, large families had to _____ in the hope that they would join together again in a new country. The situation of these refugees _____ throughout the world, and offers of help came from far and wide.

3. *physiological changes   insecticides   stimulants   terrestrial*

The _____ worked well on _____ insects but did not work as well on water-based insects.

(continued on next page)

4. *navigational guide*　　*emit*　　*exhaust*　　*arouse*　　*flee*

The hikers were lost in the mountains and worried. Their flashlights were only _____ a faint light. They had almost completely _____ their food supply. They tried using a compass as a _____ and hoped that this would lead them back to the road and safety. They finally made it. Their story of walking twenty miles in the semidarkness and with little food _____ the curiosity and interest of the public, and many news articles were written about their days in the woods.

ACTIVITY 14 **RETAINING VOCABULARY**

VOCABULARY LEARNING STRATEGY

A *collocation* is the relationship between two words or groups of words that often go together and form a common expression. If we hear or read or practice the words together often, the words become "glued" together in our minds. Try learning some word collocations.

evoke {
a response
a memory
an image
a reaction
}

mutual {
respect
trust
support
friend
acquaintance
}

Work with a partner to ask and answer the questions below.

1. At a party, what behavior evokes a positive or negative response in you?

2. What smells evoke memories of important people or places in your life?

3. Talk about one of your relationships in which there is mutual respect, trust, and support. Give examples.

4. Do you and your teacher have any mutual friends or acquaintances?

ACTIVITY 15 **BEYOND THE LECTURE: WRITING CREATIVELY**

Complete the following assignment.

Work in small groups to write a promotional brochure for a pheromone-based lotion, perfume, or cologne. Consider your target audience and what would encourage them to buy the product. Think of a catchy name to draw their attention. How much would you charge for a thirty-day supply?

FOCUS ON LECTURE ORGANIZATION

(PART 3)

Goals

- Understand the importance of recognizing lecture organization plans
- Learn about and recognize three more organizational plans used by lecturers: describing characteristics, comparing and contrasting, generalizing and providing evidence
- Learn the cues that signal these organizational plans
- Listen to and take notes on lectures that use these organizational plans
- Practice using notes to answer various test-type questions
- Expand academic and subject-specific vocabulary

In Units 6 and 7, you practiced recognizing and taking notes using six organizational plans. In this unit, you will learn about and practice three more plans.

DISCUSSION

Comparing, Describing, and Supporting Generalizations

1. In our daily lives, we frequently compare and contrast things in order to make choices. What are some things you frequently compare and contrast (e.g., food, clothes, products, movies)? Talk about one particular comparison/contrast you have made recently.

2. In our daily lives, we frequently describe characteristics (of people, places, and things). What or who are you frequently asked to describe? How do you describe him/her/them/it?

3. In our daily lives, we often make generalizations and give evidence to support those generalizations. Which of the following generalizations do you agree with? What evidence can you give to support your opinion?

   ☐ Video games are good for teenagers.
   ☐ Video games are bad for teenagers.
   ☐ The United Nations is important and effective.
   ☐ The United Nations is unimportant and ineffective.

4. Talk about a strong opinion that you have (e.g., about a social, political, or personal issue). When you express that opinion to someone, how do you support it?

Describing Characteristics

With this organizational plan, the lecturer's goal is to describe an object or living thing through its features or characteristics. In particular, the lecturer focuses on the object's physical qualities and setting.

Notes from a lecture using this pattern might look like this:

Blue Whales

Size	— fully grown	— 100 ft.
	— newborn calves	— 23 ft.
Weight	— fully grown	— 130 tons
	— newborn	— 2 tons
Color	— bluish gray	

CUES TO RECOGNIZE DESCRIPTIONS

1. Phrases or sentences that describe an object's characteristics or features:

   Concerning X's appearance, . . .
   Let's look at X's physical makeup.
   X is made up of . . .
   The layout of X is . . .

2. Phrases referring to sensory perception:

   $$X \begin{Bmatrix} looks \\ acts \\ feels \\ smells \\ sounds \\ tastes \end{Bmatrix} like \ldots$$

   If we were to visit (see, draw, examine) X, we would see . . .

3. Analogies:

   X is spiderlike (humanlike)
   X looks like . . .
   X resembles . . .

4. Rhetorical questions preceding descriptions:

   What does X look (act, feel) like?

5. Prepositions of place (and other terms) describing position:

above	*adjacent to*	*on the right/left*
below	*across from*	*in the front/back/center*
on	*next to*	*in the foreground/background*
in	*diagonal(ly)*	
over	*vertical(ly)*	
under	*horizontal(ly)*	

6. Drawings and diagrams (on the board)

Exercise

You will hear three lecture excerpts that include descriptions. The items described are noted for you. First, read the information about each excerpt. Then, while listening to the excerpt, write as many descriptive details as you can.

Example
Excerpt from a psychology lecture on the brain

Item

Description

> Brain structure shows POS. & NEG. neural pathways
>
>   - Prefrontal cortex
>
>   - POS people   — larger left side relative to rt.
>   — ↑ activity there & ↑ strength

1. Excerpt from an anthropology lecture

    VOCABULARY

    brow ridge: the raised bone structure containing the eyebrow
    cranial capacity: amount that the brain can hold

Item
Description

> Homo Erectus: 1 ½ million yrs. ago

2. Excerpt from a film history lecture

VOCABULARY

lens: a piece of curved glass or plastic that makes things larger or smaller

Item

Description

Before motion picture:

—"camera obscura"

—When light → hole in glass → projects image upside down

—

3. Excerpt from an anthropology lecture describing a typical wife's house in a Masai village

VOCABULARY

dimensions (of a space): the length and width

Item

Description

wife's house in Masai village

B Comparing and Contrasting

With this plan, the lecturer's goal is to show the similarities and differences between items. The lecturer may compare and contrast the items by first talking about each item individually and then comparing and contrasting them. Notes from a lecture using this pattern might look like the following:

> Differences betw. listening to lecture & everyday listening
>
> <u>Listening to lecture</u>
>
> Speaker/listener interaction: generally unidirectional
>
> listener — no control over direction of lecture
>
> Expectations of listener: note & retain info. for later use
>
>
> <u>Everyday Listening Situation</u>
>
> Interaction: generally interactive
>
> listener can ask for clarification, repetition, even change topic
>
> Expectations of listener: make immed. response
>
>
> ∴ Differences in interaction and expectation

The lecturer may also compare and contrast the items point by point. Notes from a lecture using this pattern might look like this:

> Differences betw. listening to lecture & everyday listening

	<u>Listening to Lecture</u>	<u>Everyday Listening</u>
<u>SPEAKER/ LISTENER INTERACTION</u>	generally unidirectional	generally interactive
	listener has no control over direction of lecture	listener can ask for clarification, repetition, or even change topic
<u>EXPECTATIONS OF LISTENER</u>	note and retain info. for later use	make immediate response

Regardless of the lecturer's style of speaking, the note-taker should try to visually represent the differences and similarities between the items. Notice that in the second set of notes, it is very easy to glance down the left-hand margin and see the *areas* of comparison and contrast. In this way, the comparison/contrast is not simply a collection of unrelated similarities and differences; rather, the similarities and differences are grouped according to topic. This is not always possible when taking notes, but it is very helpful when revising or rewriting notes.

CUES TO RECOGNIZE COMPARISONS AND CONTRASTS

1. Words and phrases that indicate a contrast between preceding and following information:

   But . . .
   However, . . .
   On the other hand, . . .
   On the contrary, . . .
   Conversely, . . .
   There were some differences . . .
   One way that it's different is . . .
   (Anthropologists) usually distinguish between X and Y . . .

2. Words and phrases that indicate a similarity between preceding and following information:

   Similarly, . . .
   Likewise, . . .
   Along the same lines, . . .
   In the same fashion (manner), . . .
   Again, . . .

3. Rhetorical questions that signal an explanation of similarities or differences:

   What's the difference between these ideas?
   What sets these apart?

4. Stress patterns that emphasize items being compared or their distinguishing characteristics:

   Now what about the women who <u>didn't</u> work outside of the home (as compared to those in the home)?

   Now the <u>employed</u> women (as compared to the women working at home) . . .

5. Body language that suggests a comparison:

   For example, hands can be used to emphasize different sides of a comparison/contrast.

on the one hand   *on the other hand*

Exercise ②

🎧 You will hear three lecture excerpts that include comparisons and contrasts. First, read the information about each excerpt. Then, while listening to the excerpt, take notes in the space provided.

Example
Excerpt from a lecture on anthropology and human evolution

VOCABULARY

fossils: the remains of ancient animals or plants that are preserved in rock

12–14 Million Yrs. Later — Fossils fr. Australopithecus (Aus.)

    Similar to ♀ & ♂ : walked upright

                        looked essentially like us

    Differences: Aus. no cranium development

                         flat from nose up (like cat)

                Aus. no chin

1. Excerpt from a lecture on philosophy

Should happiness be our end?

    Aristotle:

    Others:

    Lecturer:

2. Excerpt from a lecture on positive psychology

VOCABULARY

psychopathology: the study of psychological illnesses

Traditional psychology	This class
-more on psychopathology	-focus on
-	

3. Excerpt from an anthropology lecture on the development of societies

VOCABULARY

hoe: a gardening tool with a flat blade and long handle used to break up soil

plow: a farming instrument, usually attached to an animal or vehicle, used to break up soil

agriculture: the science of farming

Diff. betw. horticulture (digging stick/hoe agriculture) & plow agriculture

How could you rewrite these notes to emphasize the points of comparison? Rewrite them below.

Making a Generalization and Providing Evidence

With this plan, the lecturer's goal is to make a generalization and provide evidence for that generalization. There are two varieties of this organizational plan: the generalization *precedes* the evidence, or the generalization *follows* the evidence.

Most often, the generalization precedes the evidence. Such a model might look like this:

Generalization about intended topic

+

Evidence for the generalization

+

(Optional) Restatement of the generalization

In the following lecture notes, the generalization precedes the evidence:

> Correlation Exists betw. Diet & Cancer
>
> — immigrant cancer rates change to host country by 3rd generation
>
>   (even if both countries have similar pollution & food contamination rates)
>
>   e.g., Japanese immigrants to U.S. — ↓ stomach cancer &
>
>   ↑ colon cancer than native Japanese
>
>   (native Japanese diet — ↓ calories & ↓ fat)

Notice that when the generalization and evidence are organized in this way, the listener must be especially attentive at the beginning in order to understand the generalization that the lecturer is trying to make. Once the generalization is understood, the listener can relax a bit while listening and noting the evidence for the generalization.

At other times, the generalization *follows* the evidence. In this case, the lecturer leads the audience to a generalization. The generalization is presented at the end in the form of a conclusion. A model might look like this:

> **Statement of intended topic**
>
>   +
>
> **Evidence in form of anecdote(s), observation(s), test description(s), narrative(s) and/or factual detail(s) regarding topic**
>
>   +
>
> **Generalization (conclusion) based on evidence**

In the following lecture notes, the generalization follows the evidence:

> Effect of Mother's Drinking Habits on Fetus:
>
>   Experiment
>
>   Procedure: — rat's pregnancy correlated w/ human pregnancy
>
>   — at peak of brain development, rats given equivalent
>   of human alcoholic alcohol intake
>
>   Results: — offspring of "alcoholic" rats   — no diff. in body wt.
>
>   — behavioral diff.
>
>   — brain wt. 19% less
>   than control group
>
>   ∴ Pregnant ♀ should avoid excessive use of alcohol

Notice that when the generalization and evidence are organized in this way, the listener should follow the speaker's reasoning and pay careful attention to the final conclusions.

CUES TO RECOGNIZE A GENERALIZATION AND EVIDENCE

1. Words or phrases that signal a generalization or conclusion:

   So (it seems) . . .   *In conclusion, . . .*
   Thus, . . .   *To conclude, . . .*
   Therefore, . . .   *Research has shown that . . .*

2. Phrases that refer to previous evidence and signal a conclusion:

   This shows (demonstrates, implies, proves) that . . .
   Taking all of this into account, we can see (conclude, assume, predict) that . . .
   Obviously (clearly, logically), X tells (shows, demonstrates to us) how . . .
   It should be apparent (obvious, clear) then that . . .
   Based on X, we can assume (conclude, predict) that . . .
   What we have seen indicates that . . .
   This seems to mean that . . .

3. Phrases or sentences that signal evidence:

   This has been shown (proven, demonstrated) by . . .
   In fact, in recent research . . .

4. Rhetorical questions that signal evidence:

   How do we know this?   *What allows us to say this?*
   Is this true?

5. Rhetorical questions that signal a generalization:

   What can we conclude from this?
   What does this prove (demonstrate, show)?

Exercise 3

 You will hear three lecture excerpts containing generalizations and evidence. First, read the information about each excerpt. Then, while listening to the excerpt, take notes in the space provided.

Example
Excerpt from a lecture on how working outside the home affects women

Evidence

> Physical Benefits — ♀ Employed or not?
>
>   in past ♂ > heart-attack rate than ♀
>
>   Why? ♂ employed? ♀ not?
>
>   now 50% in job market but still ≠ heart-attack rate
>
> ∴ No physical benefit or risk ~ =

Generalization

1. Excerpt from a business lecture

Generalization

Evidence

> Harvard students are generous

2. Excerpt from a lecture on language learning

Evidence

Generalization

> Case of bilinguals w/brain damage
>
> — lose 1st lang. but keep 2nd?
>
> ∴

3. Excerpt from a lecture on memory

Generalization

Evidence

> Duration of long-term memory? Lasts forever.
>
> Study: Penfield: neurosurgeon Canada
>
> — pioneered neuromapping:
>
> during brain surgery, put # dots on brain, stimulate w/
>
> electricity, see response
>
> — findings?

The Near Side of the Moon (Astronomy)

Vocabulary

Related to Astronomy and Space Travel

Check (✓) the words you know. Underline the words you want to learn. Then check their meaning with your instructor or in a dictionary.

astronomy

astronaut

space station
space shuttle

manned/unmanned mission

rocket

satellite

launch

orbit

galaxy
Milky Way

stellar
lunar
solar
celestial
terrestrial

phases of the moon

extraterrestrial life

ACTIVITY **1** **PRE-LECTURE READING AND DISCUSSION**

The moon as seen from Earth

How do you think the experience of seeing the Earth from space changes a person's perceptions or way of thinking? Discuss your ideas in small groups and summarize them below.

_____

_____

When you have reached some conclusions, read the following quotes from astronauts who have been in space. What key changes in perception do these astronauts express? Were your impressions similar to theirs?

> *We are passing over the Himalayas. We can see the mountain ranges with the highest peaks in the world. At the end of the Kathmandu valley . . . I found Everest. How many people dream of conquering Everest, so that they can look down from it, and yet for us from above, it was difficult even to locate it.*
>
> —**Valentin Lebedev** (former USSR)

> *The first day or so we all pointed to our countries. The third or fourth day we were pointing to our continents. By the fifth day we were aware of only one Earth.*
>
> —**Sultan Bin Salman al-Saud** (Saudi Arabia)

> *I have been in love with the sky since birth. And when I could fly, I wanted to go higher, to enter space and become a "man of the heights." During the eight days I spent in space, I realized that mankind needs height primarily to better know our long-suffering Earth, to see what cannot be seen close up. Not just to love her beauty, but also to ensure that we do not bring even the slightest harm to the natural world.*
>
> —**Pham Tuan** (Vietnam)

> *We went to the moon as technicians; we returned as humanitarians.*
>
> —**Edgar Mitchell** (USA)

> *It isn't important in which sea or lake you observe a slick of pollution, or in the forests of which country a fire breaks out, or on which continent a hurricane arises. You are standing guard over the whole of our Earth.*
>
> —**Yuri Artyukin** (former USSR)

ACTIVITY ❷ **PREPARING FOR THE LECTURE**

The title of the lecture is "The Near Side of the Moon." What do you know about the moon? What would you like to learn about it? What do you expect the lecturer to say about the near side of the moon? Brainstorm ideas with your classmates.

 Then listen to the beginning of the lecture and answer the following question.

The primary purpose of the lecture is to

_____

_____

ACTIVITY 3 LISTENING FOR THE LARGER PICTURE

🎧 Read the following questions before the lecture begins. Then, listen to the lecture once without taking notes. After listening, answer the questions.

1. What are the two major types of surfaces of the near side of the moon?

   a. _____ b. _____

2. Which major surface type is characterized as follows? Write *a* or *b* (see above) in each of the spaces.

   ____ fairly smooth

   ____ dominated by craters

   ____ made of valleys and basins filled with molten lava

   ____ contain areas of high concentration of mass (mascon)

   ____ appear as the lighter and brighter parts of photographs of the moon

3. Look at the photo of the near side of the moon on page 142. Label each of the surface types.

4. In addition to discussing the geographic features of the moon (i.e., land formations) and the issue of water on the moon, the lecturer discusses two other major characteristics of the near side of the moon. What are they?

   a. _____ b. _____

ACTIVITY 4 ORGANIZATION

Read this summary of the lecture organization.

The lecture primarily **describes** an object by **listing** different features. While doing this, the lecturer **compares** and **contrasts** the moon's surface and the Earth's surfaces, **classifies** the surface types of the moon, and **defines** new terms.

What else do you remember about the two different surface types on the near side of the moon? Do you remember anything about how the moon and the Earth differ? Discuss with a partner.

ACTIVITY 5 DEFINING VOCABULARY

The following words and expressions were used in the lecture that you just heard. You may remember the contexts in which you heard them.

🎧 You will hear an additional example of each word or expression in a new context. After listening, check (✓) the letter of the definition that most closely matches what you think the word or expression means.

1. *perpetually*

___ **a.** lasting forever

___ **b.** occurring seasonally

___ **c.** occurring frequently

2. *distinctive**

___ **a.** common

___ **b.** special

___ **c.** likable

3. *molten lava*

___ **a.** a volcano

___ **b.** colored streams of water

___ **c.** melted rock coming from a break in a planet's surface

4. *dominate**

___ **a.** to exist in large numbers or as a major feature

___ **b.** to exist in small numbers or as a minor feature

___ **c.** to not exist at all

5. *unanimous*

___ **a.** in complete agreement

___ **b.** having unknown views

___ **c.** in complete disagreement

6. *be devoid* (of something)

___ **a.** to have relatively few

___ **b.** to avoid

___ **c.** to have none

7. *moderate*

___ **a.** to make something less extreme

___ **b.** to make something warmer

___ **c.** to make something colder

8. *twilight*

___ **a.** direct sunlight occurring around noon

___ **b.** time when the sky is lit but the sun has not yet risen

___ **c.** time when the sky is lit but the sun has already set

9. *dawn*

___ **a.** direct sunlight occurring around noon

___ **b.** time when the sky is lit but the sun has not yet risen

___ **c.** time when the sky is lit but the sun has already set

10. *attribute**

___ **a.** to regard as the cause

___ **b.** to regard as similar

___ **c.** to regard as unrelated

Listen to the lecture a second time. Take notes using the following format. The comments in the left margin remind you of the organization of the lecture.

Introduction	
Feature 1:	Surface features of near side of moon — side perpetually turned to earth
Geographic features (classification and description of surfaces)	flat lowlands (maria/mare) + highlands
Feature 2:	
Water issue	
Feature 3:	
Temperature	
Feature 4:	
Light	
Conclusions	

Listen to a section of the lecture. Then answer the questions.

1. What is the lecturer's attitude about the idea of water (in any form) on the moon?

   ____ a. He believes that if it is true, we will still never be able to mine and use that water.

   ____ b. He believes that it is impossible and future studies will prove the 1998 data wrong.

   ____ c. He is excited by the idea but believes that more research is required to prove and use it.

   ____ d. He believes that mining and using water from the moon is a possibility in the near future.

2. The lecturer says that "the ability to mine and use that water is still . . . um . . . shall we say . . . light years away." What does this mean?

   ____ a. It was done a long time ago.

   ____ b. It was done a short time ago.

   ____ c. It might be done in the near future.

   ____ d. It will not be done until the distant future.

LISTENING AND NOTE-TAKING STRATEGIES

1. Review your notes as soon as possible after listening. Perhaps there was information that you heard but did not have time to note. Add information that you remember.

2. Work with a partner to ask for information that you missed or are unsure about.

3. Consider rewriting your notes soon after listening. You can make the relationship between ideas more clear and make important ideas stand out by indenting or using headings, for example. If the lecture involves a lot of descriptions, you might want to recopy or add helpful drawings or diagrams.

Did you know?

When walking on the moon, astronaut Alan Shepard hit a golf ball that went 2,400 feet, nearly half a mile.

What was the experience like for the astronauts who actually walked on the moon? Listen to an excerpt from this interview with Eugene Cernan, an American astronaut, who, in 1972, was the last person to walk on the moon. Then answer the questions below.

1. What amazed Cernan on the moon? Check (✓) two.

   ____ **a.** The temperature extremes

   ____ **b.** The quiet

   ____ **c.** The magnificence of the mountains

   ____ **d.** The danger he was in

   ____ **e.** The dustiness

   ____ **f.** The noises

2. What was the one thing Cernan needed to make sure about before he could look around and describe things? Check (✓) one.

   ____ **a.** He had enough oxygen.

   ____ **b.** He could still communicate with the other astronauts.

   ____ **c.** The spacecraft was in good condition.

   ____ **d.** He had water.

3. Why does Cernan talk about the mountains in Colorado? Check (✓) one.

   ____ **a.** He compares the size, saying the moon's mountains are twice the size of Colorado's.

   ____ **b.** He compares the size, saying that Colorado's mountains are twice the size of the moon's.

   ____ **c.** He compares the beauty, saying the moon's mountains are twice as beautiful as Colorado's.

   ____ **d.** He compares the beauty, saying that Colorado's mountains are twice as beautiful as the moon's.

4. Why was it difficult for Cernan to appreciate the size of the moon's mountains? Check (✓) one.

   ____ **a.** He did not have the proper measurement tools.

   ____ **b.** There were no objects to help him gauge the size and distance.

   ____ **c.** He was so concerned about breathing and safety that he could not think clearly.

   ____ **d.** There was too much dust in the atmosphere and he could not see clearly.

Discuss the following in small groups.

1. When studying for tests, successful students often review their notes and try to predict questions a professor might ask. Write five questions beginning with "What" or "Why" that you might expect the professor to ask about this lecture. Then work with a partner asking and answering your questions.

   a. _____

   b. _____

   c. _____

   d. _____

   e. _____

2. Look at the picture below and discuss with your classmates what you think it illustrates. Then read the article on the next page and answer the questions that follow.

Designed by Peter Inston – London.

Moon Rooms

JEANNYE THORNTON, *U.S. NEWS AND WORLD REPORT*

In a 1967 address[1] to the American Astronautical Society, hotelier Barron Hilton invited his audience to imagine moonbound[2] tourists traveling by space ferry[3] to a Lunar Hilton with 100 guest rooms and a dining room serving everything from reconstituted[4] martinis to freeze-dried steaks.

Hilton International Hotels is keeping Barron Hilton's moon dream alive. The Britain-based chain recently hired British architect Peter Inston to design a lunar hotel. Inston says he has been talking with NASA,[5] university, and independent space scientists about the viability[6] of a resort[7] on the moon. Hilton International has spent about $300,000 so far to explore building a glass-domed inn[8] with thousands of pressurized guest rooms, galactic[9] viewing platforms, and a medical center.

Is this just a Hilton International publicity stunt?[10] Skeptics[11] point out the huge costs, complex engineering challenges, and potential safety risks. But Professor Richard S. Ellis, director of the Institute of Astronomy at Cambridge University in England, told London's *Sunday Times* he considers the project "perfectly feasible."[12] It will eventually come to pass,[13] Ellis predicted, if only to meet tourist demand for exotic[14] places to visit.

---

[1] *address:* a speech
[2] *-bound:* (*suffix meaning*) heading to
[3] *ferry:* boat going back and forth between close locations with people and goods
[4] *reconstitute:* to return something to an original condition
[5] *NASA:* U.S. government agency (National Aeronautics and Space Administration)
[6] *viability:* capability of success
[7] *resort:* a hotel with many facilities for entertainment and relaxation

[8] *inn:* a small hotel
[9] *galactic:* relating to galaxies (large systems of stars)
[10] *stunt:* a difficult or dangerous action or trick, designed to draw attention
[11] *skeptic:* a person who is skeptical or doubtful
[12] *feasible:* workable, possible
[13] *come to pass*: to happen
[14] *exotic:* unusual and attractive

---

a. What does Barron Hilton do for a living?

b. What is his "moon dream"?

c. What is Hilton International Hotels doing to keep his dream "alive"?

d. How are people reacting to Hilton International Hotel's actions?

3. A survey by the Space Transportation Association, a private organization, found that the average person would pay two months' salary for the opportunity to travel in space. Would you travel into space if given the opportunity? How much would you pay for the opportunity?

Use your notes to answer the following questions.

1. How does the lecturer define the terms below?

   a. *maria* _____

   b. *mare* _____

   c. *mascon* _____

2. Write the characteristics of the two surface types on the near side of the moon.

   a. _____

   b. _____

3. The lecturer mentions three consequences of the lack of atmosphere on the moon. Discuss those consequences and explain why the lack of atmosphere causes these effects.

   a. _____

   b. _____

   c. _____

4. The 1998 unmanned lunar probe sent back data indicating the possibility of _____ on the moon. Check (✓) one.

   ____ a. liquid water   ____ c. glaciers

   ____ b. ice crystals   ____ d. ice sheets

5. Why would this possibility be important for space exploration? Check (✓) one.

   ____ a. It would provide drinking water for astronauts on later expeditions.

   ____ b. It would be useful for growing things on the moon.

   ____ c. It could enable rocket refueling on the moon.

   ____ d. It would allow people to live on the moon for extended periods.

6. What is the temperature range on the near side of the moon?

   _____

ACTIVITY **11** **COMPARING IDEAS**

1. In small groups, compare your answers to the preceding questions. If you have different answers, check your notes and discuss your reasons for making your choices.

2. Compare your rewritten notes to the sample rewritten notes in Appendix D. Notice the organization. Is yours similar or different? Are your notes equally effective in making important ideas stand out?

Fill in the chart with the missing forms. Then choose one of the words in the chart to complete the sentences below. The meaning of the word you need is in parentheses.

VERB	NOUN	ADJECTIVE
	dominance/domination	
	variation	
	creation	
	specificity	
	evolution	
	indication	
	concentration	
	maintenance	
	occurrence	
	distinction	
	similarity	
	enormity	

1. I told him to be (exact; precise) _____ and not so general.

2. His handwriting is very (unique; different from others) _____.

3. The (great size) _____ of the project made me nervous.

4. There are certain (likenesses) _____ that we've noticed in the twins' behavior.

5. Their business is so powerful that it (shows the most influence or command over) _____ the field.

6. You need to (focus) _____ on your work more.

7. We're looking for some (imaginative) _____ solutions to the problem.

8. If people (continue; keep going) _____ a good attitude, they will increase their chances of success.

9. How often does that phenomenon (happen) _____?

10. Agriculture has (developed) _____ gradually over thousands of years.

11. Scientists have proposed (many different) _____ theories to explain the presence of ice crystals on the moon.

12. That marker (points out, communicates) _____ the location of the proposed space station.

ACTIVITY 13 **USING VOCABULARY**

You will hear vocabulary from the lecture in different contexts. After listening to each item, check (✓) the letter of the closest paraphrase of the information that you heard.

1. ____ **a.** In January 1977, Voyager 2 was sent into space.
   ____ **b.** In January 1977, Voyager 2 got lost.
   ____ **c.** In January 1977, Voyager 2 was built.

2. ____ **a.** Photographs of Ariel, one of Uranus's moons, taken by Voyager 2 in 1986, show that it has some valleys and canyons.
   ____ **b.** Photographs of Ariel, one of Uranus's moons, taken by Voyager 2 in 1986, show that its major feature is its valleys and canyons.
   ____ **c.** Photographs of Ariel, one of Uranus's moons, taken by Voyager 2 in 1986, show that it has absolutely no valleys or canyons.

3. ____ **a.** Right now (and for the next twenty years or so), there is constant sunlight at Uranus's south pole.
   ____ **b.** Right now (and for the next twenty years or so), there is no sunlight at Uranus's south pole.
   ____ **c.** Every twenty years or so, Uranus's south pole experiences a little sunlight.

4. ____ **a.** Scientists suggest a possible cause for this phenomenon.
   ____ **b.** Scientists suggest a possible result of this phenomenon.
   ____ **c.** Scientists have little idea about what causes this phenomenon.

5. ____ **a.** Uranus's atmosphere consists of hydrogen, helium, methane, and oxygen.
   ____ **b.** Uranus's atmosphere consists of hydrogen, helium, and methane.
   ____ **c.** Uranus's atmosphere contains mostly oxygen, with some hydrogen, helium, and methane.

In the lecture, you heard about *volcanoes* and *molten lava*. As you read the following paragraphs related to volcanoes, you will see boldfaced words that are common in discussions of volcanic activity. After reading, do the vocabulary exercises that follow.

The Earth appears solid but it actually contains **magma** beneath its surface. This is a picture of a **volcano**, showing some **volcanic activity**. An **active volcano** can **erupt**, sending **molten lava**, **cinders**, and **ash** into the air. **Eruptions** often come from and create **craters**, cup like depressions at the "mouth" of the volcano. Some volcanoes are considered **dormant**, literally "sleeping" (i.e., they appear inactive but may become active again). Other volcanoes are considered **extinct** (i.e., they are unlikely to erupt again).

There are often legends, myths, and superstitions related to volcanoes. Mount Fuji, for example, is an important symbol in Japanese culture. (It has been **dormant** for more than three centuries; however, it is still considered active, though unlikely to **erupt**.) The story is told that a woodsman named Visu was woken one night by a loud noise, seemingly coming from under the earth. Believing it to be an earthquake, he grabbed his family, and they got ready to run from their home. When they stepped outside their doorway, they saw that the nearby flat land had become a mountain. Visu was so amazed by this occurrence and by the strength and beauty of the new mountain that he named it "Fuji-yama," the Never-Dying Mountain.

Nowadays, hundreds of thousands of people hike to the **summit** of Mt. Fuji each year, but hikers might consider another legend: It has been said that Sengen, the Goddess of Fuji, throws from the mountain anyone who is impure of heart![1]

---

[1] From http://volcano.und.edu/vwdocs/kids/japan/japan.html, which references De Mente, Boye Lafayette. *Japan Encyclopedia*. Chicago, IL: Passport Books, 1995.

What do each of these words mean? Find their definitions in the reading.

1. *dormant volcano:* _____

2. *extinct volcano:* _____

3. *crater:* _____

Match the following words with their definition. (You may be able to guess the meaning from the context in some cases; you may need to use a dictionary for other words.)

___ 4. *magma*   **a.** the powder that is left after something burns

___ 5. *erupt*   **b.** liquid rock below the earth's surface

___ 6. *cinders*   **c.** peak, top (of a mountain)

___ 7. *ash*   **d.** to explode

___ 8. *summit*   **e.** pieces of burned substance, still not completely burned to ashes

ACTIVITY **15** **BEYOND THE LECTURE: SPEAKING AND LISTENING**

Complete the following assignment.

The Hilton International Hotel's moon hotel design team is exploring building a "glass-domed inn with thousands of pressurized guest rooms, galactic viewing platforms, and a medical center." Work in small groups to design a moon hotel. Take into account the features of the moon as presented in the lecture (e.g., temperature, water, land features, light). Where would you build the hotel? What would it look like? What amenities would it offer? What features should be emphasized to encourage people to visit? Use your imagination. When you finish, present your plan to your classmates.

Drink Your Green Tea! (Food Science)

Vocabulary

Related to Health and Diet

Check (✓) the words you know. Underline the words you want to learn. Then check their meaning with your instructor or in a dictionary.

nutrition
nutritional value

diet

malnutrition
starvation

life expectancy

health hazard
side effect
birth defect

carcinogen
carcinogenic

additive
preservative
food supplement

processed food

ACTIVITY **1** **PRE-LECTURE DISCUSSION**

Discuss your answers to the following questions in small groups.

1. What did you have for dinner last night? What did you eat that was good for you? What did you eat that wasn't good for you?

2. How much coffee or tea do you consume each day? If you drink tea, what kind of tea do you drink (e.g., herbal, black, green, oolong)? Do you think you should increase or decrease your intake of any of these drinks? Why?

3. How concerned are you about the nutritional value of the food you eat? Do you buy organic fruits and vegetables? Do you try to avoid fried foods? Do you read the labels on food products? Do you avoid foods with preservatives or chemical additives in them?

4. Do you know of any foods that have disease-fighting properties? If so, what are they?

The title of the lecture is "Drink Your Green Tea!" What do you expect the lecturer to say about this? Brainstorm ideas with your classmates.

Listen to the introduction, then answer the following questions.

1. What is the primary focus of the lecture?
   ____ **a.** Cultures and their different preferred drinks
   ____ **b.** How coffee and tea compare in terms of health benefits
   ____ **c.** Green tea and its health benefits
   ____ **d.** The health benefits of tea in general

2. What is "Camellia sinensis"? _____

3. What is the lecturer going to talk about next?

   _____

ACTIVITY **3** **LISTENING FOR THE LARGER PICTURE**

Read the following sentences before the lecture begins. Then, listen to the lecture once without taking notes. After listening, check (✓) the letters of the sentences that describe what the lecturer does.

____ **a.** Provides evidence to support the idea that "drinking green tea is good for people"

____ **b.** Provides evidence to support the idea that "drinking green tea is hazardous to one's health"

____ **c.** Talks about three different kinds of tea

____ **d.** Talks about four different kinds of tea

____ **e.** Describes the different processes used to manufacture each of the different kinds of tea

____ **f.** Describes the process of brewing a good cup of tea

Did you know?

During the Han Dynasty (206 B.C.E. to 220 C.E.) in China, tea was widely regarded as a medicinal potion.

Read this summary of the lecture organization.

> The lecture demonstrates three different organizational plans: **describing a process, classifying,** and **making a generalization and providing evidence for that generalization.**
>
> - The lecturer begins by talking about the different types of tea.
> - Then the lecturer describes (and occasionally contrasts) the different processes for manufacturing those different types (including discussing the role of fermentation[1] in the process).
> - Finally, the lecturer provides evidence for the idea that "green tea is good for you."

Do you remember anything about the different kinds of tea that the lecturer discussed? Do you remember any evidence that the lecturer mentioned to support her opinion about green tea? Discuss with a partner.

ACTIVITY **5** **DEFINING VOCABULARY**

The following words and expressions were used in the lecture that you just heard. You may remember the contexts in which you heard them.

 You will hear an additional example of each word or expression in a new context. After listening, check (✓) the letter of the definition that most closely matches what you think the word or expression means.

1. *hold in high esteem*

     _____ **a.** to dislike and disdain

     _____ **b.** to respect and admire greatly

     _____ **c.** to be unavailable or exist in limited quantities

2. *steam*

     _____ **a.** wrinkled clothing

     _____ **b.** a small body of water (e.g., a pond)

     _____ **c.** water in the form of a gas

3. *roll*

     _____ **a.** to prepare something sweet (e.g., a cake or pie)

     _____ **b.** to move a boat through water

     _____ **c.** to spread out flat and thin by using a tube-shaped object

---

[1] ***fermentation:*** a process in which an agent causes an organic substance to break down into simpler substances (e.g., yeast causes sugar to change to alcohol and carbon dioxide)

4. *humid*

    ____ **a.** dry (air or weather)

    ____ **b.** hot (air or weather)

    ____ **c.** damp (air or weather)

5. *wither*

    ____ **a.** to become smaller, less colorful, or less fresh

    ____ **b.** to smell good

    ____ **c.** to grow and produce blossoms

6. *incidence**

    ____ **a.** disappearance

    ____ **b.** unusual nature

    ____ **c.** rate of occurrence

7. *isolate**

    ____ **a.** to keep apart; to separate from others

    ____ **b.** to make animals (especially horses) sick

    ____ **c.** to cool to almost freezing

8. *inhibit**

    ____ **a.** to hold back; to prevent

    ____ **b.** to live in a place; to reside

    ____ **c.** to move from one place to another

9. *toxicity*

    ____ **a.** movement in and around

    ____ **b.** growth of life

    ____ **c.** level of poison

10. *stimulant*

    ____ **a.** a substance that is heated and drunk

    ____ **b.** a substance that gives energy or encourages activity

    ____ **c.** a substance that decreases energy or discourages activity

In addition to these words, the lecturer also uses a number of terms for different diseases related to various parts of the body. Check the meanings of the following medical terms: *lung cancer, stomach cancer, esophageal cancer* (or cancer of the esophagus), *cholesterol, tumor, dental cavity.*

Listen to the lecture a second time. On a separate piece of paper, take notes using the following format. The comments in the left margin remind you of the organization of the lecture.

Introduction

Classification and
contrast of types
of tea

Generalization   *Green tea is good for you!*

Evidence for   —
generalization

                                —

                                —

                                —

Continuing
research on green
tea

Conclusions

Listen to a section of the lecture. Number the steps in the processing of green tea in the correct order from 1 to 4.

_____ Leaves are steamed and heated to soften them.

_____ Leaves are spread out to dry.

_____ Leaves are rolled under pressure to remove moisture.

_____ Leaves are gathered from the plants

LISTENING AND NOTE-TAKING STRATEGIES

1. Review your notes as soon as possible after listening. Perhaps there was information that you heard but did not have time to note. Add information that you remember.

2. Work with a partner to ask for information that you missed or are unsure about.

3. Consider rewriting your notes soon after listening. You can make the relationship between ideas more clear and make important ideas stand out by indenting or using headings, for example. You can make the steps in a sequence clearer by numbering them.

ACTIVITY 8 **"OTHER VOICES" FOLLOW-UP**

Listen to this conversation between a student and a professor. Then answer the following questions. Check (✓) the correct answer.

1. Which sentence is NOT true?

_____ a. The student missed one test.

_____ b. The student has taken two tests and failed both of them.

_____ c. The student missed an opportunity to discuss research paper topics with the teacher.

_____ d. The student turned in a poorly written research paper.

2. Which is NOT one of the professor's suggestions?

_____ a. Meet with a counselor

_____ b. Take a time management workshop

_____ c. Go to the Study Skills Center

_____ d. Cut down on work hours

3. What does the student have to do in order to pass the class?

_____ a. Pass the next test, the research paper, and the final

_____ b. Do extra credit activities, pass the next test, the research paper, and the final

_____ c. Get an A or B on the next test, the research paper, and the final

_____ d. Meet with the professor regularly and do extra credit activities

It is important to read and listen critically. For example, this lecture reports on health benefits found to be associated with green tea. Is this information certain? Are there reasons to question this information?

Read the following excerpt from an article in the *Tufts University Diet and Nutrition Letter*. Then answer the questions and discuss your answers in small groups.

Did you know?

The earliest references to tea drinking in China date back to the year 1000 B.C.E. The British started drinking tea in the mid-1600s.

Reading Tea Leaves for Health Benefits

To date there have been no human studies in which people have been given tea and then observed to see if they develop cancers at a lower rate than others. There have, however, been almost 100 epidemiologic[1] studies in which, for example, people who have cancer are asked how much tea they commonly drank during their lifetimes and then compared to people without cancer to see if the tea drinking levels between the two groups differed. Unfortunately, epidemiologic evidence is often relatively murky.[2] People might not remember accurately enough their tea consumption[3] patterns over several decades. And even if they do, it doesn't prove that tea and not something else about their lifestyles is what affected their risk of cancer.

To make matters more complicated, the results of epidemiologic research on tea have been mixed. In some studies, tea appeared protective. In others, it seemed to make no difference. And in still others, people who drank more tea actually came down with[4] more cases of cancer.

But researchers are not deterred.[5] They feel the results vary because the studies have not been well controlled. For instance, if tea drinkers in a particular study don't have fewer cases of cancer than non-tea drinkers, it might be because they smoked or drank too much alcohol and that those lifestyle habits overpowered the beneficial effects of tea but were not accounted for. On the flip side,[6] if the cancer rates in a set of tea drinkers appear almost too low to be true, it could be that the subjects also ate diets low in fat or high in vegetables and fruits, both of which inhibit[7] certain kinds of tumors.

---

[1] *epidemiology:* a branch of medicine dealing with disease spread and prevention
[2] *murky:* dark, unclear
[3] *consumption:* what someone consumes (eats, drinks, or uses)
[4] *come down with (an illness):* to get sick with (an illness)
[5] *deter:* to stop or prevent from acting
[6] *on the flip side:* on the other hand; in the opposite way
[7] *inhibit:* to restrict movement or action

To shed light[8] on the matter in a more thorough and consistent way, the chief executive officer of the International Epidemiology Institute in Maryland, William Blot, M.D., says, "We need more and better controlled investigations in humans." And he believes such investigations are worth conducting. The evidence from studies thus far is encouraging enough, he says, to "provide incentive[9] for additional research to understand the role of tea drinking in a healthy diet."

Dr. Mukhtar, the skin cancer researcher at Case Western Reserve, agrees. He says that by giving tea to a high-risk group of people, such as those who have skin cancers removed yearly, a lot could be learned about its ability to protect against sun-caused tumors. That would be much more telling[10] than asking people who already have cancer how much tea they used to drink. Once tea's efficacy[11] is proven, which Dr. Mukhtar believes is only a matter of time, he expects to see its active ingredients incorporated into suntan lotions, over-the-counter cosmetics, even shampoos.

Of course, no matter what might eventually be confirmed about the benefits of tea, switching from, say, coffee to tea is never going to take the place of eating a relatively low-fat diet with plenty of vegetables, fruits, and whole grains, nor is it going to replace several days a week of vigorous[12] physical activity. Like oat bran, tea is just one food that, included in a lifestyle that's healthful overall, may provide a bit of an edge[13] in staving off[14] chronic[15] diseases of aging.

[8] *shed light (on something):* to make (something) clearer
[9] *incentive:* motivation
[10] *telling:* revealing important information
[11] *efficacy:* effectiveness; ability to produce the desired result
[12] *vigorous:* energetic
[13] *edge:* advantage
[14] *stave off:* to prevent
[15] *chronic:* repeated; continual

1. According to this article, what concerns should people have about studies claiming that green tea improves health?

2. According to this article, what types of studies need to be done?

3. What conclusions do you think the author of the article wants you to reach about health regarding tea?

4. Do you plan to change any of your personal habits based on information you heard in the lecture or read in this article? If so, what do you plan to do? If not, why not?

ACTIVITY 10 USING YOUR NOTES

Use your notes to answer the following questions.

1. The lecturer describes three kinds of tea. Decide which characteristic is related to which tea. Check (✓) the appropriate box for each characteristic.

	GREEN	BLACK	OOLONG
a. It's the least processed tea.			
b. It requires semifermentation.			
c. It's the youngest tea.			
d. It's allowed to oxidize for the longest time.			
e. It's the freshest tea.			
f. Its processing takes about 3 hours.			
g. It accounts for 4% of world tea production.			

2. True or false?

_____ **a.** All tea comes from the same plant group.

_____ **b.** Black tea turns black because it is burned.

_____ **c.** About 75 percent of world tea production is black tea.

_____ **d.** The studies showing reduction in cancer of the esophagus were done in Japan.

_____ **e.** A cup of green tea contains more vitamin C than a cup of orange juice.

_____ **f.** A research team in the United States found a substance in green tea that may help protect against dental cavities.

_____ **g.** Green tea contains the same amount of caffeine as coffee and black tea.

3. According to Japanese research, drinkers of green tea have lower rates of which of the following? Check (✓) all answers that apply.

_____ **a.** Cancer of the esophagus

_____ **b.** Stomach cancer

_____ **c.** Depression

_____ **d.** Skin tumors

_____ **e.** Blood cholesterol

_____ **f.** Breast cancer

_____ **g.** Lung cancer

_____ **h.** Heart disease